'Did I ever tell you? – I married him for his elbows.'

THE BUTLER DID IT AGAIN!

Peter Westbury

The Butler Did It

Westbury Heads South

Peter Westbury

© Peter Westbury, 2016

First published in 2016 on behalf of the
author by Scotforth Books

ISBN 978-1-909817-31-9

Typeset in Bell 11 on 13 by
Carnegie Book Production
Carnegie House
Chatsworth Road
Lancaster
www.carnegiepublishing.co.uk

Printed and bound by
Blissetts

To past Loves; and to my far-flung Family
who should have become accustomed by now to
Westbury surfacing from time to time.

Foreword to an entertainment

WHY DO WRITERS CHOOSE TO write under a nom de plume? It happens rather a lot and famous names come readily to mind, from the three Georges – Sand, Eliot and Orwell – to Robert Galbraith a.k.a. JK Rowling in recent years. They had their reasons and I have mine.

The idea of "Westbury" came to me during a mid-life crisis while I was re-inventing myself at the School for Butlers in London. I thought it would be an excellent tactic if, on graduation, I adopted a new identity to suit the role I was about to play. It was simply that.

When I eventually came to write my memoirs, it helped that the central character already had a fictional name with the resulting freedom to write pretty much what he liked in the first person singular. It was a name, furthermore, that opened up title possibilities, starting with Westbury Meets East and continuing now with Westbury Heads South.

I have developed a fondness for Westbury; he has become my scapegoat and regularly gets a ticking off when I forget something. Since my retirement he has still had his uses.

It must be obvious to most people that a butler's profession, the second oldest in the world, exposes him to all manner of privileged information, not to mention sights that could be described as being of a private nature, just in the course of doing his job. To his employers he is invisible most of the time, blending with the furniture and expected to be just as discreet. In this, the second memoir, there is a temptation to reveal secrets. We'll have to see.

Westbury is growing old disgracefully, still depicting himself as a bit of a ladies' man. He has been accused in the past of an inclination to fantasise but we have to realise that, were he ever to resort to that, it would be purely in his quest to entertain; a good enough reason to indulge him, in my opinion.

It would be fair to assume that a few of the names have been changed to protect the guilty but by far the majority of the characters you will meet are of a good-natured or amusing sort whether hidden behind an alias or not.

In any case, what's in a name? Just as long as it's a good read…

P.F.S.

Contents

The Butler Did It

Westbury Heads South – Part One

Introduction

SCENE ONE
The Library, Moyns Park, 1998.
It is early May; sunlight is streaming through the French windows. The butler has just entered the room.

BARON: Ah Westbury! There you are!

BUTLER: Yes, Baron.

BARON: I shall be getting married again…

BUTLER: (*sotto voce*) You have my commiserations, Sir.

BARON: (taking no heed)…in two weeks' time. You'll need to go to Klosters and set things up. Take the secretary with you – she tells me she's got some German; here's a chance for her to prove it. And I want you to go ahead and arrange the civil ceremony but the future Baroness has insisted on a religious blessing of some sort so you're to rope in a Roman priest or someone who can carry it off. Judith [his interior designer] will help you but I want you to keep a close eye on expenses. I'll give you a list of 40 guests plus her mother and some sisters that I'm flying out but their accommodation, which you must find in the town, will be down to them. Make that perfectly clear to the hotel people as well. I'm expecting you to come up with something out of the ordinary by way of venue for the reception. I said unusual not expensive. Book your own flights now and I want a daily progress report. As soon as we have a firm date you can organise the travel for the guests. I, of course, will be using the private jet. That's it. Above all – watch the budget."

BUTLER: Thank you, Sir.

Chapter One
How The Other Half Lives

THINGS HAVE MOVED ON APACE since my return from Japan and I am now running the household of a man with a dream. He has acquired the imposing but run-down dwelling that sits in a 400-acre estate on the Essex/Suffolk borders and previously belonged to a cousin of Her Majesty the Queen. From my own home base I have moved geographically east, but in every other sense it could be said that I've "headed south" or downwards. The house, part Tudor, part Elizabethan, part Georgian and all parts shabby, needs a good deal of money spending on it and this is reflected in the staff wages. Compared to Bridewell Heath I find myself in very reduced circumstances but that doesn't make for much of a book title.

Moyns Park

The Baron is very driven, his enthusiasm at the initial interview, which took place in his suite at Claridge's, was most contagious. The crazy thing is (I can say it *now*) he is determined to have it up and running in the *Elizabethan style!* So, NO motorised transport, NO electricity, certainly NO plastic. The kitchen garden is to be restored, the stables to be revived, the furnishings simplified, the modern [David Hicks] wallpaper stripped off to expose the lime plaster. We are to make our own beeswax, soap, candles, clothes, food, warmth *and* entertainment (if there is any time left). I had heard, following the interview, that he is known to the Gentlemen of the Press by the unflattering title of "Baron Bonkers". This was due to some unfortunate investment mistakes he made when the bottom dropped out of the dotcom market and boom turned to bust. I thought to myself "Wait till they find out the manic nature of his *new* venture!" I say "manic" because it had become clear that the dream had not taken into account two major anachronisms: the intrusive Stansted flight path by day and the glare of the nearby town's sodium streetlamps by night.

Well, to be fair to both the Baron and myself, his enthusiasm *had* proved infectious to a large number of job hopefuls from whom he could take his pick. I did need to get back into employment and at butler level there was not much being offered. [I'd been to Grosvenor Place to Lord Andrew Lloyd Webber's office for a preliminary interview but the prospect of working in a London basement did not thrill me and his Lordship is renowned for his tantrums.] When I enquired about the accommodation I was told there was a comfortably furnished room at Moyns Park on the servants' landing that had been left exactly as it was when the Mountbattens' butler occupied it *and* it had a bathroom for my exclusive use. As it turned out, the décor was not at all to my taste but the plumbing worked and it had the best view of the gardens. And what is wrong with helping someone to realise his dream, however eccentric?

But, I have rather jumped ahead…I'm always doing it.

§   §   §

Outside the Musée d'Orsay

Westbury Meets East closes where I and the delectable Miyuki are on a Cathay Pacific flight out of Tokyo and via a Hong Kong stopover to Europe. We each had a return air ticket with a question mark hanging over it. While our future was anybody's guess we had the very agreeable prospect of nearly two weeks together, firstly in Paris and then in London.

Well, Paris of course worked its usual magic; why shouldn't it? Our hotel room had private access to a rooftop terrace and a view of the Eiffel Tower. [We were only a stone's throw from the rue de Grenelle, but it was not the time to go calling on Venezia! (see Westbury Meets East p.159)]

The Butler Did It

The Musée d'Orsay, an old favourite, was revisited and Miyuki led me to the Salvador Dali Museum over in Montmartre which I must have walked right past without noticing on any number of occasions. It's a bit tucked away but really worth seeking out. This was July and our visit coincided with Bastille Day and the famous *défilé*. Being so petite, Miyuki had a grandstand view of the procession sitting on my shoulders to see over the crowds. Romantic evenings and blissful nights ensued; on a *bateau mouche* excursion we both fell asleep..

Iconic view taken from the OXO Tower

London, the city I know best, was enormous fun, unmatched as it is for all-round entertainment. It was my delightful companion, though, who through her research had lists of things she wanted to do and places to see and it is thanks to her that we found ourselves taking lunch on the balcony of a recently opened restaurant, the OXO Tower on the South Bank overlooking the Thames with a fabulous view of some of the most iconic architecture in the world. On another day we took the Tube to Finchley Road and found our way to the Sigmund Freud Museum. Her interest took me by surprise; she didn't strike me as symbol-minded at all. She loved Kew Gardens and the charming park behind Hogarth's House at Chiswick. And on our last day we climbed the steps inside The Monument to enjoy a panoramic view of the city in which I've worked and played for going on half of my life.

After eleven days of western food and european language my delightful companion was ready to return home. None of my leads in the quest for another job in Japan had amounted to anything concrete and so our parting became inevitable. Tears were shed at Heathrow.

§　§　§

I re-registered with the agencies and set to work on the manuscript that became *Westbury Meets East*, the diary account of the life, loves and misadventures of a British butler in almost permanent culture shock as he copes with the running of Bridewell Heath, an expensive caricature of an English village with manor house, boarding school, hotel and pub, craft house, a babbling brook (with concealed pump) linking two ponds (with orchestrated frogs on a timer) and accessed through a pair of grandiose wrought iron gates in the picturesque but unlikely setting of the Japanese mountains. (See the Book for plan and photos). It was truly amazing, like something that had started as a folly, developed into a film set and then grown larger than life. It was right up the butler's street!

§   §   §

In November I found myself at Heathrow airport again waiting, slightly apprehensively, to greet Sashiko the distractingly pretty air hostess who I had first met when curiosity drew her to that anomalous village in the foothills above Shirakawa. In spite of my work-load we had managed to enjoy some private time together by arranging to meet surreptitiously at the viewpoint overlooking Lake Hatori whenever I could slip away. She became a frequent visitor and a mutual attraction grew. Then one particularly memorable afternoon was spent showing her Nanko Park; this is not a euphemism – things *were* getting serious. After further increasingly amorous dates she announced that she wanted to have my children. Now *here* she is in England, full of smiles and very excited. This is one resolute lady and very desirable, too.

In the car she explains that back in April she had arrived at Bridewell Heath expecting to find me available [I was in Sabah at the time with Miyuki] and the days had seemed long before contact was possible again. She knew I'd be continually on the move once I'd left Fukushima. Anyway, she says, everything's fine now and nothing has changed: she still wants to have my children.

We arrive at the Wiltshire cottage where we start to focus on the purpose of her visit and all the time I'm thinking of how much trouble and expense she has undergone in her determination to reach me – surely only a cad would mention the vasectomy now! She's flown all this way with one thing foremost in her mind. I can't possibly disappoint her. Actually, I wonder why it is that I always take people so literally? Perhaps *wanting to have my children* could be taken as a euphemism; and with that thought I felt much more relaxed.

She was eager to be baring her shoulders for me for the first time; she regarded them as her best feature and coyly left them covered until last. It is no exaggeration to say that she was lovely all over but it was her obvious joy when she slowly and finally revealed her

The Butler Did It

unforgettably beautiful shoulders that made for an extraordinarily erotic moment.

We fitted in a lot of focussing in those few days and nights, leaving the house only twice – once to visit Lucknam Park Hotel a short distance away because we were getting hungry and the other time to make a hurried call in at the British Museum Shop to buy some souvenirs to back up her story of a strictly didactic sort of trip to Europe. [Which description turned out to be closer to the truth than she envisaged I am sure because, thanks to what I learned during that time with Sashiko, ladies' shoulders began receiving the fullest appreciation and closest attention.]

All too soon it became time for us to part. She left with the sheets off the bed in the bottom of her suitcase. How romantic is that?

§ § §

January 1998 saw me at Claridge's for the interview in which the dear Baron outlined his plan to re-impose the Elizabethan way of life on the estate on the Essex/Suffolk borders which he was in the process of buying for a little over one million pounds. A striking young lady emerged from a bedroom. She was unusually tall and clad head to foot in black leather. We were not introduced but I was later to play a key role in her life of which *she* would be totally unaware but which *you* may successfully deduce if you have been paying attention. At that time they were not yet engaged.

The Baron did seem keen to take me on but in spite of regular reminders I was not to be included on the payroll until April, as it was said that the property contract had taken ages to complete. One other member of the new staff, the land steward, and I met at the London Office and were taken in the Bentley to see our new workplace. It had quite a history, from receiving a mention in the Domesday Book to receiving Ian Fleming as a guest who came there to write. (In parenthesis, one of its more recent owners, Ivar Bryce, was supposed to have been the inspiration for James Bond. I've just added him to the list.) In the 1570s one Thomas Gent started to turn it into a residence appropriate to a courtier – he was a baron of the Exchequer – and benefitted from the moat which still surrounds the house on three sides. After additions by one Gent generation after another, the house one sees today resembles, in plan form, the shape of a squared-off U, the Tudor and Elizabethan architectural styles flanking the Georgian facade. We approached by the tradesman's entrance, of course, but the exterior aspect was really impressive, from the gate-house to the stable block, its twenty or so loose-boxes and its clock-tower, the walled garden and the estate houses. The elevations of the Main House were magnificent. The interior was another matter. And behind the kitchen garden walls was devastation.

One week later I was delivered in the same motorised vehicle as my effects and entered discreetly by the back door.

§ § §

Baron Carel Johannes Steven Bentinck, for that was his name [Bentinck derives from the Old Germanic name of Bento, which happens amusingly to be Japanese for 'lunchbox'; he was always ready to eat.], wisely left us alone to find our way around and see what needed doing. A map of the interior would have been useful. There were changes of level where the houses joined; main staircases and backstairs; doorways concealed as bookshelves; everything except a priest's hole. None of it furnished, with the exception of my bedroom and the billiards room. I headed up an initially basic staff of six dealing purely with domestic matters. John the Land Steward had his office above the stable block with Fiona as secretary plus a book-keeper. He also had charge of the gardeners comprised mostly of the old originals as well as a young man with aspirations to becoming Head Gardener – although I'm sure it was his pretty wife who nailed them the job, recruited by the Baron as a pair "for their enthusiasm". For my part I had inherited the existing Housekeeper who came in each day from the village. As a matter of fact I found her rather daunting, certainly very possessive of her territory, but the Baron wished to keep her on for the time being at any rate in order to tap into her local knowledge. [Rule 2 in the International School for Butler Administrators handbook: do try to get on with the Housekeeper and the Secretary.] Two others on my team had joined on what was *their* understanding that they would be in the running for Housekeeper and Assistant Housekeeper in due course. Competitiveness had quickly begun to show but both of them had definitely been chosen on looks. Tentative questioning showed no likelihood on the part of the incumbent to move over. How interesting. So for the moment we had two of them tripping over each other for the title of Assistant Housekeeper. One of them was the other half of the married couple whose husband was expecting to become Head Gardener. Situations have a habit of solving themselves and so it was proved just a few weeks later. The enthusiastic hopeful let his pruning skills run amok on a rare climbing rose, whose fabulous blooms completely hid the Old Dairy so you'd hardly believe there was a building there. Apparently photographers flocked here every summer to snap this rarity in its glory. Anyway, the precious plant died. The Baron was furious and sacked the young man who promptly left. Which was actually a pity for the Baron and I'll explain why.

Going back a bit, the telephone rang one day (how are we going to manage without *that*?!) telling me to expect delivery of two horses before the end of the morning. [Rule 1 in the Butler's Handbook: expect the unexpected!] The horses, a colt and a filly, were a gift from the Baron's stepdaughter. I'm convinced we could have had more notice. We had two hours in which to prepare two of the disused stables and to fence off two paddocks because the young and frisky horses had to be kept apart. I was pleased to hand this problem over to John who quickly sourced some straw and animal feed from a local farmer whose tractor rolled into the drive just as the horse-box arrived.

Dehlia, the nice smiley Filipina cook, who, together with Billy Bueno her handyman husband, had been poached from the Bentinck pad on Mallorca, produced from nowhere a light celebratory lunch for the visitors and the Baron, of course, was delighted. He was in residence sporadically, turning up frequently without notice – well it *was* his bat and ball, after all – but he had arrived on this occasion driven by Moralee his personal valet/chauffeur (another member of staff who'd been poached, this time from Alnwick Castle, the Duke of Northumberland's home that was later made even more famous as the location for Hogwarts) which took the pressure off me more than somewhat. The Baron announced that he intended to have an early morning canter whenever he was at Moyns Park.

Fortunately for John, who would otherwise have had to find a stable-boy from the village, one of the Housekeepers-in-waiting, keen perhaps to find favour, volunteered to get up extra early to tack up the lucky horse in readiness for the gallops. She had claimed to have had experience and a love of horses and to my great relief did pretty well because my own experience at a riding-school in my mid-twenties has resulted in a lifetime's respect for the creatures (calling it 'fear of' would be more truthful) and if I had the choice I preferred to keep my distance.

I was usually up with the lark myself and caught an occasional glimpse of the stocky well-built rider on top of the plucky little mount. Think Thelwell pony cartoon. All concerned were happy until one morning no-one appeared to saddle up the colt. The acting stable-girl had quit the evening before without a farewell; together with her husband, the sacked gardener.

I was getting to like Baron Bentinck who maintained his slightly roguish smile through most trials and tribulations. He was a stickler for politeness at all times and at every level.

Little by little we learned of his colourful past life. For example, he told us he'd spent

He was a stickler for good manners at all times.

Good mooorning, Baron!

a year as a *gaucho* in Argentina – hence his horsemanship of which he had an obvious pride. Which, sadly and perhaps inevitably, came before the fall. He was thrown. He made light of it but he was clearly in pain and couldn't walk properly for quite a while.

§ § §

I took the shuttle train one day from the airport to Liverpool Street and thence to SW3 where Sir had his headquarters. It was a tedious journey and I'd not been looking forward to the traipse back. However, after the meeting the Baron kindly invited me to travel with him in the Bentley; he wanted to make one of his impromptu visits. I sat in front of course with Moralee, the chauffeur-cum-valet. In the back with the boss was a military looking chap I'd never seen before. Introductions were made and he turned out to be a new member of staff, some ex-army wallah engaged to be the Baron's *aide-de-camp*. He'd even kept his Army rank, Lieutenant-Colonel or something. I'm never impressed when ex-service personnel carry their titles into civvy street. I mean, I never *ever* use "Corporal Westbury".

During the journey I could hear the Baron taking calls on his mobile 'phone which he'd thoughtfully switched to vibration mode. Every so often we'd hear "What's happening?" [I began to be able to impersonate his voice quite well.] Then a reply, followed by an instruction. Back in SW3 he had someone on the staff permanently in front of a screen monitoring the exchange rates of the world's currencies. "Not a bad morning, Westbury", he said when he stepped out of the car. "Made sixteen hundred pounds on the way here."

The chauffeur had pulled in to the car park of the local village inn as instructed. It was very quiet – long past lunchtime for normal people. I thought "Fat chance." The ex-soldier marched inside and came back out with a smile and a swagger. "They're fixing something for us." I could have strangled him. We filed in. The lunch was pleasant enough and the group was more relaxed; especially the Colonel whose cheeks were now flushed with the alcohol. His confidence increased and he became more and more chummy with the Baron. I remember thinking "That's not going to go down well."

At Moyns the Baron went on his usual prowl closely followed by the newcomer. Rather too closely, I sensed; the boss was looking a bit edgy. Far worse than the false *bonhomie* towards me, was the "old-pals" nudging he was giving the Baron. That won't do at all – the Baron is related to the Queen, for goodness sake. [Through the Cavendishes.] There was something about this chap that didn't ring true – just a feeling I had – a slight nervousness that I'd met before, characteristic of those who live on their wits. [I wasn't wrong. He was indeed ex-Army but, unknown to the Baron he'd been cashiered, his career shortened due to his excesses with alcohol. Honestly, I don't know where the Baron finds them!] He didn't last long; about as long as the hapless gardener. He took the Bentley home one weekend while the Baron was abroad and was seen giving rides to his neighbours. This placed young Moralee in a very embarrassing position but as the valet was valued much more highly than the adjutant, it was the disgraced Colonel who was sacked and the over-familiarity curtailed at a stroke.

§ § §

Life was becoming a bit routine after the initial novelty of my surroundings. Up early, breakfast with the staff in the kitchen (Dehlia did a wonderful Eggs Benedict), then off to show a good example by helping with the wallpaper stripping in the Great Hall. At this stage the place was still empty of furniture and hangings (drapes, etc., not punishments) so there was little requiring my attention on a daily basis. The Baron insisted on camping out with a mattress on the floor (which is probably why we saw nothing of his young lady) and Moralee dealt with all his other needs. I drove into Halstead from time to time on an instruction to hunt for unusual beers but only twice found labels that were unfamiliar to the boss.

So when the summons came to go to Klosters to prepare for the wedding I was really ready for a change of scene. Fiona, too, had begun to scratch around for things with which to look busy and not too keen to scratch at wallpaper, though she did help a little. In her early thirties, she was really very attractive but, like a lot of shy girls with good figures, had a tendency to round shoulders. With better deportment she could have been a fashion model. I was looking forward to working more closely with her in Switzerland. As it turned out, Judith had booked Fiona on the same flight with her and I flew out from the City of London airport in the seven-seater Citation II with the Baron and one of his chums who spent the whole time in the air playing the money markets. As the second flight officer was in charge of refreshments there was nothing for me to do – except pinch myself every so often.

Cessna Citation II

Situated a short distance from Klosters, Chalet Eugenie was the Bentinck family home. [Among others. There was the house in Knightsbridge and the villa on the north side of Mallorca where the £5 million replica of Errol Flynn's yacht 'Zaca' was moored with a crew on permanent standby. Plus there were the family-owned hotels. There may have been more.] This huge chalet which I'd hoped would help solve at least some of the needs for accommodation, was undergoing seriously extensive alterations and would not be anything like ready. From this moment on it was "The good news is…" followed by "The bad news is…". Plenty of capacity in the town's hotels. But, right between seasons, the town's hotels were all closed for the month of May. Yes, it would be possible to stage the wedding reception in the Nature Reserve. But, sorry, no access allowed to motorised transport other than maintenance vehicles. Well the Baron had stipulated something unusual but I couldn't imagine the bride and groom and their guests arriving on tractor-drawn trailers. There was a lot to sort out.

It was clear at our first meeting that Fiona's German had suffered from lack of use. Ever, probably. Unknown to me, however, Judith spoke it fluently. Well there's a real bonus. Let's get cracking with our lists.

The ladies took on the hotel proprietors and persuaded sufficient of them to re-open four days earlier than planned. They booked the Town Hall for the civil ceremony and then went on the hunt for a cleric of no matter which denomination to perform a blessing. I, meantime, tried to figure out a way of pleasing the Baron with something "different but not expensive" for his reception. There was just one building in the pretty wooded park, a brick-built cowshed no longer used. Not large, not in itself pretty, but it could be masked with foliage and awnings to increase the amount of shelter in case the weather turned unkind. The concrete floor was covered with evidence of past bovine occupation but once scraped and hidden with fresh straw, could look quite bucolic. How to solve the problem of tables and chairs? We'd need quite a lot. If we maintained the rustic theme, perhaps there'd be time to get local carpenters to knock up some long tables and benches. And we could ransack garden centres for plants in flower to give colour to a glade I'd spotted nearby, a suitable place to have the blessing. Mental note to try and borrow a couple of *prie-dieux* from one or other of the churches.

Transport! How were the bride and groom and eventually the guests plus helpers (not many of *those* in evidence) going to get from the Town Hall to the reception venue, a distance of nearly a mile? How do summer visitors manage to tour the Reserve? They can't all be walkers. *That* was the answer. Somewhere I'd seen a poster showing horse-drawn carts. We've got to make enquiries.

We organised enough horses-and-carts with their drivers so that, spaced at a suitable distance apart, once they had dropped off their passengers at the cowshed they could circle back to the park entrance to pick up the next in line.

With the catering decided upon and arranged with two of the town's *Gast-statten*, we just needed permission for deliveries to be made. Tractors and trailers were fine for the wooden furniture and the decorative stuff but what about the luncheon supplies? Fortuitously, one of the caterers was a councillor and they waived the rule to enable the food, drink and tableware to be delivered hygienically in vans.

That left the matter of the cowshed floor. Nothing for it but to borrow a shovel and get on with it.

§ § §

Actually, I was still strewing straw over the bare concrete when I heard the horse-drawn carts drawing near. The Big Event was about to start so on with the motley! Feeling really and truly uncomfortably warm, I slipped into my best tailcoat to hide the signs of my efforts and went to greet the first wagon. Blow me down if it wasn't bloody Moralee waving merrily from the head of the procession! He'd arrived three days before and had been lying low.

§ § §

As with most social occasions, it is only the organisers who are aware of the glitches and it was the same in this case. Nothing had gone seriously wrong and the Baron was well-pleased, especially when everything was totted up next day.

"Ah! Westbury, *there* you are!" said he, grinning from ear to ear.

"Yes, Baron."

"It didn't turn out so badly after all."

"Thank you, Sir; that *is* a compliment."

"Well here's the thing. The Baroness and I would like you to take a break…and join us on honeymoon."

"Well that's frightfully kind, Sir." (Oh lor'.)

"No, not entirely. I'm convinced they're overstaffed at my mother's… [It's the house on Mallorca. She is bedridden with 24-hour nursing care and on the way out. Perfect atmosphere for a honeymoon.] …and I'm sure you'll agree when you see the situation. Lot of spongers.

So, bring Fiona for company if you like. Why not? The Baroness and I will be leaving this afternoon, as you know. Get Moralee to drive you to Zurich when you've cleared up here and we'll send a car to collect you from Palma. See you there in two days from now. That's all."

What a blow! On top of which, I later discovered that someone had stolen my bowler. My second best, too, the one with the red satin lining.

In Memoriam

I was *so* cross. I didn't know which was worse. Well I did, actually, because the bowler *was* replaceable. On reflection, a few days on Mallorca with the lovely Fiona wouldn't be bad.

§ § §

And so it came to pass. Understandably, I had a very lukewarm reception at the house, the staff were barely polite. Their morale was rock-bottom. Their comrades in the kitchen, Dehlia and Billy, had already been transferred to England, it was *their* jobs that were now under scrutiny and they recognised me as 'The Undertaker' (even without the bowler hat). The stay would have been extremely uncomfortable but for the presence of Fiona. Each morning we walked the short distance to the little *poblado*, took our time over our coffee and walked the long way back along the coast. That part I didn't mind at all.

What I did mind and minded very much was the discovery on returning to Moyns that the Baron had given instructions to demolish my living quarters during my absence. I found my belongings in a cupboard in a bare bedroom. This was part of his overall plan to remove completely the partitioning in the uppermost storey so as to make space for ladies to take their constitutional indoors during inclement weather as they had been able to do in bygone days under the attic roof. I'd like to know where all these ladies were coming from. The Baron was becoming more than a niggle to the people at English Heritage with his cavalier attitude to the rules concerning Grade I listed buildings. Actually, if I hadn't been the "victim" in this instance I would have probably thought this a perfectly legitimate operation in terms of restoring the *status quo*. Most curiously, they were even more incensed over his stripping the Great Hall of its hideous wallpaper. And I *was* pleased to have helped him with *that*.

However, I regarded the underhand demolition of my bedroom and downgrading of my personal circumstances a very poor reward for my part in organising his wedding *within a fortnight*. With time, the reason for all the rush became apparent to me, as it had already been clear to pretty well everybody else. Their relationship had been turbulent, the engagement on then off, on again then off, for months. But she had trapped him ultimately in the time-honoured way.

The Baron accepted my resignation. I had been with him for two months. It seemed longer.

Postscript: Moyns Park, which had been acquired for something over £1 million, was on the market with Strutt & Parker in October 2001 for £7.5 million. It went for £6 million in 2002 – not a bad profit in three-and-a-half years. One-hundred-and-fifty of the four-hundred acres were described as "being converted to organic". This was probably the nearest the Baron got to creating his Elizabethan Dream.

Lisa, Baroness Bentinck née Hogan, his second wife, gave Baron Steven Bentinck (third ex-husband of Cairo-born Princess Eleanora Czartoryski) three children. She filed for divorce in 2005. After years of acrimony a settlement was agreed in 2011.

Brinley Moralee left the Baron's employ in 1999 to better himself. He found a position in Eire with Irish nobility. He was joined shortly afterwards by the Buenos. You could say it was a case of "the biter bit" or, as they say more poetically here in the Périgord Noir, "*l'arrosoir arrosé*".

I have often wondered what became of John the land steward who I liked very much. He didn't say a lot but worked all God's hours to cope with the mountain of stuff the Baron threw at him. I'm perfectly sure there was more to him than met the eye. I don't know how I came by the idea that he'd farmed somewhere in Kent and gone bankrupt; the nineties had been tough on a lot of people. I do know he had a wife; and two boys at public school. It's not difficult to understand how much he needed the job and why he kept his eye on the ball eighteen hours a day seven days a week. From his pallor you could have thought he worked in a library instead of on the land. It may be fanciful to think it but I had the feeling that perhaps the Baron had some hold over him. He went home for just one short weekend – from Saturday lunchtime to Sunday evening – while I was there. He loved mealtimes in the kitchen with the domestic staff; the quips and the wisecracks and especially the sense of family which I'm sure he missed enormously. Of course that applied to me, too; but I'd had longer to adjust. What became of him when the Baron sold up? I have no idea. Maybe he reached retirement age.

I did stay in touch with him for a while; it fell to him to find my replacement. They interviewed applicant after applicant. He kept asking the agencies "Why can't you send me someone like Mr. Westbury?" I could have told him. They won't find that person because for honesty, conscientiousness and good-humoured anticipation I am unmatched. This is not boasting – this just happens to be a fact.

As for the butler – or house steward, as the Baron insisted upon? Well, he reached his 60th birthday on June the 21st, unemployed. Who will have him now?

§ § §

I cannot now remember the name of the agency in Kensington behind the V & A that found me my next job. It was run by the owner, a very chic and attractive divorcée in her early forties. ["A dangerous age, Cynthia!" Unquote.] Halfway through August the 'phone rang with the excellent news that I'd been accepted for the position of butler to a Chinese millionairess in *Kuala Lumpur.* Yippee! The office explained there might be some cooking involved until the matter of a replacement for the chef was resolved. Was that OK? Fine, absoluteley fine. "Good, then I'll tell them they can post you your air-ticket." Marvellous. I wouldn't mind getting to know Kuala Lumpur better. I'd heard there had been major improvements to the air quality.

4

Unlucky for
some

Two days later the Chinese lady's secretary telephoned me direct to say very apologetically that there'd been a change of mind. When the boss lady had noticed there was a four in my address, regarded by Chinese as an unlucky number, she took it as a bad omen and decided differently. 8 is their number of choice where good luck is concerned because the karma has no way of escape. Which is not at all the case with the number four where there are four open ends for the luck to leak out. Load of old nonsense really. If there was any "leaking" involved it was probably on the subject of my cooking.

§ § §

Back at the typewriter, *Westbury Meets East* was shaping up and I started sending sample chapters to literary agents. It was the end of September 1998 when the very personable owner of the Staff Agency came on the line again this time with a job offer in Italy. I found out much later that she had told the people that she fancied me herself, which no doubt intrigued the Signora and landed me the position – on a trial basis! So I headed further south: to Tuscany.

Chapter Two
The Italian Job

THE "TRIAL BASIS" WAS SOMEWHAT unexpected. A couple with two German Shepherds were looking for a butler who the dogs might find acceptable! Although I had emphasised "dog-fearing" in the modest list of my shortcomings, it was known at the agency that I badly needed to get back into employment so, as this was all there was, it had been arranged for me to undergo a month's trial to see if the dogs and I proved compatible.

At Pisa airport, the rather majestic lady advancing on me slowly but purposefully at the arrivals gate with all the dignity of a ship berthing turned out to be Signora Velotti, the American wife of my new Italian boss. I followed her distinctive walk out to the Mercedes and she drove us the shortish distance through the tunnel – which the wealthy northerners of Italy wish will one day mark the dividing frontier with the far poorer South and the sooner the better – and on to the Villa at San Lorenzo di Vaccoli on the outskirts of Lucca.

Two huge dogs came bounding out of the rose garden to inspect the new minder. I braved their frothing mouths and foiled their attempts to knock me over by hiding behind their mistress. When they finally calmed down, I remembered the old claim about dogs resembling their owners – their manner of walking was practically identical to the slow bouncing gait of the Signora.

The Villa Velotti

I was shown to my quarters and then introduced to the Dottore, a slightly built man with girlish eyelashes and a habit of looking skywards over your head when speaking to you. We established terms of address: they would call me "Westbury" – my choice not theirs as they had been used to calling their previous butler by his first name; imagine! – and he would be "Dottore" and his wife would be "Signora" (again my choice; she had been used to being called "Hillary" by staff in the relaxed American style). They were very welcoming, I must say, but it didn't take long to realise that I was replacing the only previous living-in staff, a man-and-wife team and for the present there was no sign of a housekeeper, footman, valet, cook or maid. Five gardeners came in from the village to tend the gardens and orchards as the seasons required, but they were not my responsibility.

As the month drew on (I had avoided the dogs as much as possible), some of my duties were taken over by a newly appointed housemaid from nearby who came in her own car daily to do the cleaning and lunchtime cooking. Her name was Armida and the impression I had was that she got the job because they'd had an Armida before who had been excellent. Her eyelashes looked as though they had spent the night in curling tongs which gave her a misleadingly flirty look because she was really quite a dragon.

By the end of October I was told I had the job.

§ § §

This was not his first exposure to Tuscany. In a previous life, long before Westbury took over on this butler career, he had come in the summer of '92 to the outskirts of a town near Siena to learn how to fly a hot-air balloon. He really caught the bug and this would be an appropriate moment to share that adventure and subsequent others . What follows are extracts from his File on Tuscany:

September 1992

    There is glare off this page as I write! I am sitting outside in warm sunshine at a rustic table - actually an old door, still with its nailed-on hinges, lock and bolt-keep. It makes a challenging eating surface, never mind writing-desk, but perfectly complements the weathered portals of this old farmhouse that has been my home for the past week. No longer a working farm, it must have been great in its heyday. The coat of arms of the Count Roberto Guiccardini, who owns the Castello di Gargonza at the end of the lane, is represented in relief in the stone lintel above the entrance. It is now the only grand thing about this place but it serves well as the oficina for this Hot Air Ballooning enterprise and as living-quarters of one Robert Etherington who is its operator. He is a pleasantly eccentric Englishman of indeterminate age but undoubted skill when it comes to piloting his range of baskets of varying passenger capacity, each with its distinctive and highly colourful hot-air inflatable envelope.

Diary: 8th to 15th September

Martedì. 10.30 flight out of Stansted destination Firenze. With an accident on the M40, congestion on the M25 and a further accident on the M11 my heart was racing as I parked somewhat untidily in the short-term car park and hared into the terminal building to learn that, following a departure delay, passengers had only now started to board. I could still make it. The very obliging check-in lady printed my pass while 'phoning her colleague in the waiting lounge. "You will have to carry your suitcase, Sir, as the baggage hold has been closed but they will be waiting for you." I thanked her profusely and seeing that they were now expecting me at the gate, I had time to grab a bottle of brandy from the duty-free shop on my way through the smart almost brand-new and beautifully clearly signed airport. My heart-rate returned to normal somewhere over the Appennines.

Florence, and no sign of R.Etherington Esq. I realised very soon how dependent I am on him, not just for transport but language, too. Eventually his abused-looking maroon Toyota jeep rattles to a stop. Its ancient look is due to being one of only four prototypes built aeons ago; it is very possibly the only survivor and as we noisily bomb along south of the city and on to the *autostrada* in the direction of Arezzo, it is clear that the manufacturers wasted no money on comfort; but as my father would say, a third class ride is better than a first class walk. Robert is late because he is in the middle of a retrieve, explaining that he has left his "crew" in a bar – a German guy from Mainz called Andreas – and would I mind lending a hand? With what? We reach the bar only to discover that Andreas has pushed off; we will have to manage the retrieve operation by ourselves. I pay for our drinks and the German's lunch as well and we drive on. With help from the farmer in whose field the balloon had landed and who has already given Robert two kilos of tomatoes, we set about loading the jeep.

[I'd like to just mention that, at that time in Italy – and I do hope that things have not changed – it was regarded as an honour to have a balloon land in your field. In England the landowners used to rush out of their houses to demand a landing fee.]

Fully loaded, so that my suitcase must sit on my lap, we head off to Monte San Savino with its really beautiful old centre, thanks in part to some sympathetic restoration. Robert is hailed by many of the locals as we stroll through the town, trades-folk mostly, occasionally stopping for conversation in fluent Italian. [I realised, long afterwards, that it was highly probable that some of them were reminding him that he owed them money.] But I particularly notice Anna-Maria, a really gorgeous young fashion designer and Nella, a teacher from Napoli and very much hope that our paths cross again. We also bump into Andreas who has hitched a lift to the town and thence to Gargonza.

We all drive out to the farmhouse and "the deal" is explained to me. Shambolic is the colloquial word that best sums up the situation: bed and board of a very basic sort in keeping with the laid-back nature of mine host whose four-line advertisement in the Daily Telegraph was sufficient to tempt me into this adventure without revealing much in the matter of actual details. [When I told my wife that I had booked myself a week's holiday hot-air ballooning in Italy, she thought it was madness. I retorted that she seemed to think it alright for her to go off sailing. To which she replied: "Well, at least I am able to swim. *You can't fly!*"] I'll have a roof over my head and I'll fork out for some of the provisions. While Andreas is barbecuing the meat that I bought in Monte San Savino, Robert and I are making inroads into the brandy and lemonade. I feel better already.

Mercoledì. Nella, whom I met briefly yesterday, and her daughter Aurora are booked for a flight at 7a.m. It is Aurora's birthday and I have offered to take photographs of the launch. Apparently, it is a matter of local gossip and therefore by definition unsubstantiated that in Naples, Nella was house-keeper to a priest and that Aurora is theirs. She and the little girl live alone, there is no paternal figure in the vicinity and nothing can stop tongues wagging. They manage.

I have some time to myself and decide to explore the surrounding Tuscan landscape. Lovely aromas of pine, mint, basil and much more that D. would identify immediately. By 11 o'clock the clouds have built up and there is a resulting overcast atmosphere. I head up to the *castello* with my camera. This *piccolo villaggio* is divided into holiday apartments but it is the tail-end of the season and very empty. The part that was the castle is like a poor man's *parador* but there is a pleasant enough *ristorante* and utterly delightful garden and courtyard.

Back at base-camp the crew jeep returns and Robert prepares the *pasta*. Nella is bringing the *pesto* sauce she has made and is to join us for lunch. This is a long drawn-out affair and eaten indoors at the table under the window with the castle view. She leaves and we get ready to drive to the Strauss concert outside Rignano sull'Arno on a *fattoria* [farm]. Food was advertised but does not materialise. I meet and chat with Gabriella – an Italian teacher of French – and her friend Flavia who also speaks French. Also Donatella – the Italian names are so musical. The concert is packed with too many people in search of free entertainment and food and wine; like us! And the music was, well, Strauss.

Giovedi. Weather rather misty so no flight.

At about 12.30 the 'phone rings and we are invited to lunch at Anna's. [It turns out that she is Anna-Maria's senior partner in their fashion *laboratorio.*] We had just sat down to our own *spaghetti suggo* prepared by Robert and me! One day you miss out entirely on supper, the next day you get to eat two lunches! I soon realised that this is very much how Robert lives. And so as well as lovely Anna, we meet Nicolo her son, Silvio from Innsbruck, plus Fulvia and Vittoria from Milano. Anna's reclaimed, restored house is just delightful: south-facing, simply furnished with much charm. We eat outdoors. Prosciutto and melon; a bread and vegetable soup; and an egg-based white pudding not unlike *zabaglione.* Wine a-plenty and coffee.

The weather improves as we sit over lunch and Robert announces that he and I will take off from the launch field just below the farmhouse in the early evening. So exciting.

A rapid ascent. Up and away to the east, the castle in fine view, the lake, Monte San Savino, the wind carrying us quickly now, over and well clear of the motorway, the eventual descent to land in the twilight north of Terentola. Only thirty minutes duration but it was so exhilarating. Radio contact with Andreas had been spasmodic but now with darkness looming there was some concern. He'd most probably "lost" his way and "found" a bar. From which he eventually emerged.

We wind up in a *pizzeria* and I am so elated I buy the *entire* crew their supper! Robert is anxious to have my impressions and we talk and talk while the drinks keep coming. Friends of Robert, Fabrizzio and Giuliano join in and it gets quite late. Not that I'll be able to sleep. I'm on too much of a high and there's still tomorrow morning's flight to look forward to. It is a balmy evening and, as we drive home, from the tape-deck in the jeep come the strains of Mozart's Piano Concerto No. 21, the perfect sound-track

Venerdi. Up at 6.30 for a 7a.m. start. By 7.35 I am standing in the basket next to my pilot and buddy Andreas. It is extremely calm. Our ascent has been almost vertical as there is next to no wind. The early cloud cover has totally dispersed and visibility is marvellous. The *castello* looks magnificent; I feel such a lucky b. We hover almost motionlessly, then change altitude in search of a breeze. We drift very, very gently in a different direction to that anticipated...

The Italian Job

After two and a quarter hours of gentle floating above what could be some of the most beautiful scenery in Europe – viewed, at times, from about five thousand feet in our search for some wind – we are absolutely static above the walled-town of Lucignano.

Lucignano – looking for somewhere to land.

Andreas ponders the situation as we are almost down to reserve level in the fourth – the last – cylinder! There are three open spaces below us: the schoolyard, the *cimitero* and the *immendezzaio municipale* – none of them really options!

We are descending towards the dump, reasoning that it is there we'll do the least expensive damage, when a whisper of air carries us sideways and we just avoid colliding with the picturesque centuries-old town wall. A promising-looking field looms but the bad news is that the sunflowers have been harvested by hand and the stubble is left pointed and sharp. Andreas brings the basket gently down and when he gives me the word I jump down with the tether and pull the whole shebang past the hedge and into the next field where it is safer to land and deflate. There's some delay before Robert appears with the jeep. He has had to be tractored out of a ditch. The obliging farmer has followed with Lucia his small daughter who is delightfully inquisitive and keen to see the equipment up close.

Once they've departed we pounce on the picnic: red wine, biscuits, cheese and tomatoes. Andreas refers to it as a "second breakfast" but I have no recollection of having had the first one.

The return along the lovely winding roads we have seen from the air includes a stop to refill the cylinders with LPG and another at a village bar for something further to eat to keep us going as lunch will be late. A poster on the wall of a castle reads "For Sale" £1 million. And so we head on back with Andreas and me sat on top of the jeep,

The Butler Did It

the passenger seat being occupied by a huge demi-john liberated by Robert from the tip!

Among the new faces around the lunch table today are Toby and Caroline, friends of Robert over from New York. Toby plays viola and by popular request recites the story of Ferdinand the Bull to viola accompaniment. I was hearing it for the first time and it was a real *pièce de résistance*. Then someone called Liz arrives from near Siena. She writes children's books and has come to sketch and paint and to crew for Robert when Andreas leaves. A rather gawky hockey sticks type, I wondered where she was going to sleep because the only room with a spare bed was mine! I needn't have worried: she moved in with Robert.

We all get ready for the drive to Incisa for a Schubert concert. It takes place in a gem of a house in the spacious music-room. Again, it is over-subscribed but while waiting for the musicians to arrange themselves, I sit strategically next to Adriana and Giulia to make their acquaintance, which gives me the pleasant duty to go and fetch them drinks in the interval. And I realised afterwards that by going round the back to the kitchen there was no queue for the food. I served them – and me – and later, when it was all over, stayed behind in the otherwise emptied concert room with three extremely well-dressed ladies listening to a young man playing jazz standards extemporised on the grand piano. Magic! Much more my cup of tea. What a treat! What a day!

Sabato. Breakfast up at the castle – Robert, Liz, Andreas and I. Then Robert and Andreas leave to set up a "tether" for someone who is promoting the re-opening of his hotel and to whom Robert owes a favour. I make a picnic lunch for self and Liz who is painting in the walled garden where we sit under the pergola and put the world to rights. A wedding party has hooted its way past the *casa colonica* for a photo-shoot in the castle grounds. The bride and groom come down the steps towards us. She is rivettingly beautiful and my *"Buona fortuna"* is rewarded with a flashing smile and a *"Grazie"*

With a siesta behind us we smarten up and drive to the hotel in tiny Castelmuzio where the balloon appears incongruously among the rooftops. In our host's private dining-room we are surrounded by centuries old frescoes. The hotel is owned by Marcello and his wife. He could be a Medici descendant; they have such strong faces these people; each might be peering at you from a framed portrait in the Italian School section of the National Gallery. I lost count of the number of courses; much wine, much hilarity.

It is Andreas' last night and he is in no hurry to leave – I wonder why?! Robert and Liz are to stay over so that they are in position for tomorrow's launch. Andreas and I return, breaking the journey at Lucignano for a nightcap. We cannot resist climbing up into the old walled town through the archway into the narrow streets to the church over which we had flown the previous day; unexpectedly emotional. 1 a.m. and so peaceful, hardly a soul abroad. Special. *Domenica*. Fantastic purple/orange dawn. Waved Andreas off. Up for breakfast in the *castello* dining-room. *"Vorrei fare collezione, per favore. Cafè con latte e susca pompelo."* There are just two guests in the room – Trevor and Joan Jones, South Africans who have emigrated to Twickenham – the only sound is the crunch of toast which makes us laugh and we finish up sitting together. My suggestion that they might like to consider a balloon flight is well-received. I'll check with Robert and let them know.

All was set up for the following evening and I returned to the castle to advise them. Trevor was on his way to shop in Monte San Savino and said I was welcome to tag along, which was lucky as the brandy stocks needed replenishing. We ran into a monumental traffic jam! And the cause? The *"Sagra del Porchetta"* – the Pig Fair – sounds so much prettier in Italian.

Had a beer together, as much to enjoy the atmosphere as to satisfy our thirst. Trevor asked if I'd be free to spend the day tomorrow in Siena with him and Joan. I cannot believe my luck! And when he adds San Gimignano – good gracious! Fabrizzio and Giuliano look in at the bar as we are about to leave so of course we are obliged to to linger longer. Fabrizzio gives us each a brochure of his paintings – what a talented guy: painter, poet, film-maker, etc.

Back at the farmhouse a family of four has arrived for their morning flight: John Murphy, a Milanese editor, Adriana his wife and the children Roberto and Sara. Trevor is sent by Joan to ask me to join them for supper at the Torre de Gargonza which is fine by me. Then during the meal Robert appears to say that they are dining with the Murphys at the *ristorante* on the top road and why don't we meet up for a sharpener when we've finished. Which we do. *Fennet Branca* is a new experience for me – a sort of lethal Owbridge's – proposed by the Joneses. [I believe they were the importing agents for South Africa.] We all pack in round the farmhouse table afterwards and it starts to get late. Fabrizzio pitches up around 1 a.m. He is getting to be a mystery man; we are in the backwoods here and he can hardly be passing by as it is a no-through-road. However, he joins in the story-telling. We run out of sharpeners and the party breaks up. *Lunedi*. Everyone is up early for the Murphy family take-off and I prepare for the Siena trip. Soon we are travelling through *Toscana profonda* searching for the Villa d'Arcena that the Joneses are keen to see. It turns out to be a recently-opened very up-market hotel that had once been the manor house to the surrounding vineyard estate. Very elegant and lavishly furnished, it exuded luxury. A belvedere had been added at roof level and overlooked a beautiful swimming-pool in the immaculate gardens. We headed on to San Gimignano, a truly amazing place: just thirteen towers remain from the original seventy-six. We saw wonderful interiors and courtyards glimpsed through ancient doorways; a great feeling of history in surprising contrast with some very modern abstracts displayed in the art galleries. [I had no notion as to how my life was to change so dramatically and so soon. The next time I found myself here was when I had the pleasure of showing my daughters around when they visited me in Lucca in the summer of 1999. But that is part of another story.]

On to Siena. Walking through the narrow streets inside the walls on our way to the cathedral and the Campo, it was clear from the posters that the *Palio* had been held here two days earlier. There were still many visitors about, though and restaurants were full. Eventually, we found a family-run place for our *pasto del mezzogiorno* which was on me. Afterwards, Joan treated us to a slice of *panforte ricciarelli*, a chewy almond-flavoured confection for which this *citta* is famous. Then we went to the *Museo del Duomo* to see 'La Maesta' by Duccio di Buoninsegia and on to the roof to take photographs of this most picturesque town and imagined what it would be like from the air. [I returned in July 1995, on leave from Japan, to fly again with Robert and Liz, who were then installed in the *quartier vecchio* of Rapolano Terme, and I was able to write in my book – 'Westbury Meets East': "Siena seen from a hot-air balloon has to be one of the most enduring mental snap-shots of this very self-indulgent holiday".]

We are back in good time for Joan and Trevor's early evening flight but on Robert's return from refuelling he has to make the decision to cancel because of a cloud build-up. All are disappointed and I feel terrible for having wound the Joneses up to such expectations. As the *ora di cena* approaches the idea of eating together at the *trattoria* on the top road receives all-round approval and we proceed there to raise our glasses and our spirits. It is my last night in Tuscany. I settle my account with Robert before retiring to bed. There's not enough lemonade for a sharpener each so we finish the brandy neat.

Martedi. The others leave for the early morning launch – dreadful couple from Rochdale – and I pack my bag and wait for the Joneses who have very kindly offered me a lift with them to Florence so that I can spend some sight-seeing time in the city before my afternoon flight. I listen one more time to what has become known as the "Elvira Madigan" Andante with a lump in my throat. What a week! Who'd have dreamed that it would culminate in a walk along the Arno and across the Ponte Vecchio? [And how could I have ever predicted that, through an unimagined change in my personal circumstances, I would get to know Florence well some seven years later while working in San Lorenzo Vaccoli on the outskirts of Lucca. Ten years later still, retired and living in France, I happened to pick up a book – "A Party in San Niccolo" by Christobel Kent, set in atmospheric

Florence – my pleasure heightened by being able to call to mind the exact locations and, maybe, even some of the characters!]

I leave Trevor and Joan [who, years later, moved out of congested Middlesex and into Sweden's forested countryside] at 1.15 and take a taxi to the airport where my flight is delayed by one hour but, no matter… it was thanks to a flight delay that I made it here!

The perfect weather conditions showed off the snow-topped Alps, Mont Blanc and Lac Léman very recognisable. Breathtaking. Stansted, by contrast, was overcast with a slight drizzle . *Tipico!*

Postscript. This adventure proved to be the first of many, for I had become completely hooked on what, for me, was a completely new sport. I stayed in touch with Robert and we flew together in Italy several times. No two flights are the same for obvious reasons. One led to an encounter with two contessas when we landed in the grounds of their *palazzo* which was absolutely crammed with art works, from framed Jean Cocteau drawings to sculpture by Henri Gaudier-Brzeska. They invited us in and proposed dry white wine – it was about nine-thirty in the morning. I noticed one of them wasn't drinking and went to pour her a glass. "Gee, no thanks, not for me," came her response in a Kentucky accent. "I've just had two gins and tonic!" It turned out that she had married her Italian nobleman between the wars. Mother and daughter were both full of tales of a grander age. On another occasion, flying low over the *crete* which is a weird uniquely contoured landscape near Siena, Robert excelled himself, using his knowledge of the behaviour of the ground wind to manoeuvre the basket along and around the curves, an extraordinary skill you would not believe possible.

§   §   §

Diversion. In return for crewing, I subsequently enjoyed many a flight with a local private balloonist over the beautiful Thames valley scenery of Berkshire and South Oxon. Richard and his chum Terry kindly included me in the team for several memorable escapades: to London for the Cross City Event – in which the "special shapes"

The Butler Did It

included a huge bowler hat and a giant rolled up Financial Times; to Dover Castle for the Cross Channel Race using the roll-on roll-off ferry for the retrieve; to the Bath Festival Meeting launching from Victoria Park; and most exciting of all, to Chateau d'Oex for the January Rally in the Swiss mountains with the snow deep and crisp and uneven.

Andreas, too, had stayed in touch and at my request drove down from Frankfurt with his balloon trailer to meet me and my brother in Weilheim, not far from Munich, where we had gone to celebrate his 50th birthday, staying at the house of an old school friend. The plan was for five of us to take to the air: my brother, our friend, his wife, myself and the pilot. When Andreas clapped eyes on our chum who had expanded impressively in the ten years or so since last we'd met, he insisted that four would have to be the maximum so Dick announced his wife would be the one to drop out. The small matter of who was going and who was staying became more and more academic as, day after day, we awoke to abysmal weather conditions with no prospect of a flight. Until, on our very last evening, a Sunday, with a glowering and unsettled sky, Andreas made the decision to launch from a field on the edge of the village. Each of the small helium balloons had been carried in a different direction. "But dat's vott you get mit mountains!" said Andreas. At this point Dick looked like chickening out. His wife, though, was chuffed at the chance of taking his place; but Dick would have none of that.

The next hour and a half were among the most hair-raising of my life, though there would be much less hair to raise these days. We were flying over dense forest. Nobody had a local map and in any case there were no roads below so the retrieve vehicle, driven by Andreas' young and inexperienced cousin, quickly lost visual contact. The wind was taking us every which way and the sky grew angry. It started to rain. Staying airborne wasn't too much of a problem although the burners seemed to be doing overtime. Time passed and no sign of a possible landing place. There were fire-breaks in the forest beneath but none wide enough for us to land in. Goodness knows where the cousin in the retrieve vehicle had got to; radio contact had been lost in the folds of the mountains. Andreas

Chateau d'Oex January Rally

The Italian Job

had switched to the reserve gas cylinder as the rain increased. The light was also failing and we were in urgent need of a flat open space…

Just beyond the next ridge a field came into sight! We began the descent and our pilot began shouting landing instructions: "You must bend zer knees!" But the wind current increased as we got closer to the ground so we were no longer losing altitude but moving at speed horizontally just feet above the not very flat field so that, when the basket touched the ground, it turned over on its side.

The radio-telephone flew out of Andreas' grasp and was later found smashed. But *he* had the softest landing because he fell on top of my fat friend. In fact, we landed twice and then were dragged along for a distance of roughly 100 metres. It would have been further but for the ditch, invisible from the air, which acted as a brake.

"Stay in zer basket!" shouted Andreas. "I vill tell you ven to ged out"

He righted the basket by using the burners and one at a time we climbed out as the balloon deflated. We were lucky to get away with a few minor cuts and eventual bruises. I left them to start the packing up and made my way in the dark down a track in the hope of finding a house with a telephone but I hadn't gone very far when I came across a man sitting in his car. He was a taxi-driver on his day off!!! The hunting season was due to start the following week and he was checking out the terrain! Better still, he was pleased to be of help and drove me to Dick's address. The cousin had sensibly returned to base when he lost all contact with us and the taxi-driver piloted us back to the field, refusing payment. Aided by the head-lamps of the three vehicles – Dick's wife had followed in her 4 X 4 – we loaded up all the gear and stood around in the rain with glasses of champagne singing "Happy Birthday To You" and not wanting the adventure to end.

Ironically, I am finishing these reminiscences by remembering making contact with a Japanese balloon pilot who was appointed organiser of international meetings such as those in Albuquerque and Metz. I had just arrived in Fukushima and expressed my interest in flying and describing Brideswell Heath [c.f. "Westbury Meets East"] as the perfect setting, which it was, weather permitting, for launching a hot-air balloon.

He prevaricated and prevaricated, which is what the Japanese do excellently well. He arrived with a balloon crew three years after my first contact and just as I was leaving for good. I'm still trying to think of a polite word that describes him adequately.

§ § §

Wind the clock forward six years to the Villa near Lucca where gradually things fell into place and I became accustomed to living in this time capsule. It could have been the setting for a Henry James novel. The fourth wall to the vast living room-cum-hallway supported the very elegant main staircase. A full-length portrait of a lady hung in the angle near the foot of the marble steps. She was referred to as the Contessa, the implication being that she was an ancestor. All very romantic but the bullet holes were false for sure. The room itself resembled a furniture showroom, explained, as I found out eventually, by the fact that the Velottis had run a successful antiques business in Atlanta. Presumably they brought with them a lot of the leftover stock when they came over. It was eclectic to put it politely. Elton John had been one of their clients.

There was a covered terrace on the roof of the extensive library built behind and parallel to the house. This and the patio sheltered by a vast fig tree were used in the summer for entertaining of which there was to be quite a lot. Fine-mesh netting had been installed to prevent the figs from dropping on the long table and the Signora explained that candles were lit in glass jars along the paths in the early evening before the arrival of the guests. They had two enormous electrified altar candlesticks to stand at each end of the serving table. This sounded like a lot of work but I looked forward to being involved in creating this lovely atmosphere for the guests. [I must have covered several kilometres in the course of those evenings because the kitchen was a considerable distance away but it was good exercise and the Velottis were always appreciative.]

The work was mostly routine without being tedious. The reason it wasn't boring was because of the amazing location and the kindness of the boss and his wife. There weren't many rules, in fact I can only remember two: toast was always to be served with the *formaggio* and no drinks were to be served to them while they were using the *piscina*.

§ § §

In my capacity as chauffeur I did the regular weekly shopping but also the out of the ordinary shopping such as buying bottles of 90° proof alcohol available off the shelf from the village grocer as needed when the season for making *limoncello* came round. I drove the Dottore to his wine merchant and although I was only watching on the sidelines I learned a lot. Obviously we weren't there to buy the likes of Soave, Bardolino or Valpolicella. What I had already noticed in our cellar was a quantity of Sassicaia and Tignanello, both local wines that I'd never heard of. Neither of these Tuscan wines has a DOC or even a DOCG. Well here's a thing – Sassicaia is rated by many as Italy's finest red and commands huge absolutely stratospheric prices. It's a similar story with Tignanello. These "butler years" have really brought home to me 'How The Other Half Lives'. [In 2015 a bottle of 2012 Tenuta San Curido Sassicaia was priced at $179; the 1985 at $2898.]

After the olive *raccolta* – the estate included an impressive-sized olive grove big enough to be registered as one of the *artigiani* (small growers who produce a combined total of up to 3000 litres of oil each year) – I drove behind the truck to the Frantoio di Matraia with four of our *giardini* as extra manpower. Once our yield had been weighed (396 kilos) we were in a queue for the pulping, squeezing and screwing by disappointingly modern machinery. Finally the liquid was filtered, purified and bottled. Our batch made just short of 50 litres. Quite an eye-opener. And it *is* a bit special to be cooking with your own olive oil.

When the Velottis went abroad it was he who drove the Mercedes to the airport and I brought it back. They were great Anglophiles, enthusiastic patrons of the arts and flew frequently to London.. The National Gallery benefitted by their sponsorship. They funded two exquisitely illustrated catalogues to complete a definitive series on European Schools of Painting. Neil MacGregor was Director at the time and was invited to come and stay.

And of course I had the pleasure of escorting the German Shepherds to keep their regular appointments at the beauty parlour. Without Armida to help me I'd have been flattened crossing over the road between the car park and the *salone*, not by traffic (though the Italians *are* mad drivers) but by the two excited and powerful dogs enthusiastically tugging on their leashes. Between us we managed them; one at a time. [Dog-handling is now covered in the new butler apprenticeship scheme started up at Blenheim Palace…]

§   §   §

On my day off, usually a Sunday unless it conflicted with other things like the to-ing and fro-ing of guests, I could take the car and drive in any direction that took my fancy. That is how I discovered little by little the joys of Viareggio, famous for its *passeggiata* (evening promenade) and the thickest hot chocolate drinks; Portovenere, the picturesque seaside town associated with Byron, Shelley, Wagner and Georges Sand and now a Unesco Heritage Site; the Cinque Terre perched on and in the cliffs above the Golfo di Genova; and Montecatino Alto, the prettiest of places tucked above the commercial spa town of Montecatino Terme – all easily managed there and back in a day. And the thing is, I could see all these gems outside of the busy tourist season. Wonderful.

§ § §

I have an anecdote about Georges Sand. In February 1964 while on honeymoon in the Baléares, my bride and I were visiting Valldemossa and being shown round the monastery where Chopin had stayed. The only other people requiring an English-speaking guide were two Americans. She was bossing him around and taking lots of photographs. "Say, Frank, why don'cha come and stand by the pyano. Gee, Frank, jus' look at his tiny hands!" And Frank would obediently shuffle here and shuffle there as commanded. Our guide was doing her best to be heard and had just reached the fact that Georges Sand had also been a visitor. "Hey, Frank," interrupted the woman, " d'ja hear that? Georgie Sands was here!" and then, to us "Y'know, the American comedian!"

I thought I ought to gently put her right. "Actually, it was Georges Sand the French writer."

There was a pause and then a disappointed "Oh, HIM!!"

§ § §

I did lack companionship. The lunch out that I invited Armida to share one Sunday under pressure from Signora Velotti was an embarrassing disaster and not repeated. The Velottis seemed very sympathetic to my situation and very generously made the guesthouse in the grounds available to any family visitors that I would like to invite. I must say I was overwhelmed. Looking at it from the outside it seemed rustic but once inside you would never have believed it had once been a farm. The interior was de luxe and chock-full of antiques and precious objets d'art. So I had the pleasure of inviting my brother and sister-in-law on one occasion and my daughters on another. As my employers were absent on the first occasion it was like a holiday for me as well and I was able to include the further flung delights of Florence, Siena and San Gimignano on their sight-seeing itinerary as well as my favourite places nearer at hand.

§ § §

Portovenere

The
Cinque Terre

Monterosso al Mare

Vernazza

Manarola

The Butler Did It

Corniglia

Riomaggiore

Among the other guests who came to stay in the luxurious farm, two stand out in my memory. The first was Ms Gloria Hunnicutt, actress turned television presenter, delightful company and full of show business anecdotes. I remember one story she told against herself. It was a live programme. Alan Rickman had already been announced. Throughout the interview she referred to him as "Rick". He didn't bat an eyelid. She didn't find out until it was all over. When she apologised he laughed it off. "Just remind me in future to call you "Honey"!

The other memorable visitor was the owner of the Staff Agency whose name I still cannot recall and who, it may be remembered, had told Signora Velotti that she thought me fanciable One day after supper at the Villa she asked if I would go down to the guesthouse later when I was off-duty to have a word.

I knocked on the door and went in. She wasn't wearing very much and what she was wearing she had let fall open. She poured me a drink. We exchanged a few pleasantries and soon ran out of conversation. Then, with a grin

"Well now. I got you the job!" A pause. It was easier to agree.

"You did. And now here we are, representing the two oldest professions in the world and neither of us quite sure of the protocol…!"

You may be in no doubt that I behaved as a gentleman should. That is to say, unhurriedly and with due consideration for her feelings. And mine.

The
Guesthouse

§ § §

The Butler Did It

Spandex Ballet-dancers!

Poster

Another example of their generosity was when I conversationally mentioned that I'd had the wish for a long time to one day attend a production of Aida in the world famous Verona arena. They gave me two days off in a row to make it possible. Tremendous. They even found me a convenient hotel about 200 metres from the entrance. What an experience! The singing, the drama, the spectacle, the atmosphere, the traditional lighting of candles; and that was just in the hotel.

In Act III, On the Banks of the Nile, I couldn't make out where the splashing was coming from. The set designer had raised the level of the stage so that a long water tank could be concealed underneath and exposed when needed to form a canal on which boats could really float. Ingenious. For this very untraditional *percezione*, a huge blue pyramid had been constructed centre-stage surrounded by short square columns and scaled-down "Cleopatra's Needles", all very geometrical (see overleaf). Made possible by the hollow floor, some actors made unexpected entrances from out of the top of the columns propelled by tiny lifts. And the *corps de ballet* was completely sheathed, heads and faces included, in batwing silver Spandex djellabas. The whole effect was extraordinary.

§ § §

AIDA – the Verona Arena Stage setting.

For the first Christmas we had a VIP to stay in the shape of Signora Velotti's mother who had arrived from Atlanta. Of indomitable appearance she had an endearing sense of humour and was very appreciative of my little treats. Accompanying her were a husband-and-wife team, that is to say her resident cook/houseman and her companion/nurse. We got on fine.

Come the actual Christmas Day morning, the news was broken to us that we were to have the day off. I suppose they thought it would be nice for us or perhaps, for a change, they liked the idea of having the villa to themselves. Scarved and buttoned up against the cold, the three of us set out to see what the chances were of us finding somewhere for lunch at such short notice. Very slim as it turned

The Butler Did It

out. There was hardly a soul about and you could see why – there wasn't a commercial premises open of any kind. Hardly surprising. We trekked through the grey canyons of Lucca systematically finding nothing and just as we were about to give up the search we saw a light in the window of a small *trattoria*. We peered inside at the uninviting looking flagstone floor but the owner grinned and gestured to us to come in. He and his wife couldn't have made us more welcome. It was wonderfully cosy inside and we were soon tucking in to a warming *risotto*. Our luck was in after all and it was a Christmas none of us is likely to forget.

§ § §

In Italy, food is uppermost in the mind of the waking population. As you would expect, there were plenty of seasonal vegetables from the garden and one of the gardeners regularly brought in a whole *pecorino* from his brother's caves where it had been maturing. The Signora went annually to Paris for a course at the famous Cordon Bleu cookery school, held by me in low esteem having crossed swords with two of their graduate chefs whilst in Japan at Bridewell Heath. In truth Signora Velotti had no real need to go – she was a wonderful cook – but she went up in company with a girl-friend for a week and by all accounts, hair was let down.

Naturally, at the Villa, Italian-style cooking predominated but it was by no means pasta with everything. I ate what they ate but smaller helpings in between serving the larger ones in the dining-room so it didn't do my digestion much good. Nevertheless I was converted, learned a lot and have continued to enjoy making the simpler dishes ever since.

If you're not besotted with *risotto* then you should maybe try '*risotto al tartufi*'. Of course it would help if you are based near Lucca. For dinner parties you can telephone your order to a delicatessen within the walls and then send the butler to collect it. Allow him plenty of time for chatting up the delectable *signorina* behind the counter; or anywhere else.

If you do ever find yourself in Lucca it's worth making your way to the Buca di Sant'Antonio (St. Anthony's Hole!). It's a *ristorante*, not far from Puccini's birthplace, at 3 via della Cervia. And if you are lucky enough to be there in October just after the grapes have been harvested, their menu includes an extraordinarily fine dish – '*faraona all'uva bianca*' (guinea-fowl cooked with whole white grapes) – a gastronomic miracle. In my opinion.

This city of Lucca is a phenomenon. For centuries it deterred any attempt at all at invasion with its impregnably thick walls; and it remained so until latterly when it has become the target of tour operators. It attracts huge numbers in the summer so it is best to avoid the congestion if there is a choice. Narrow streets draw you to an oval-shaped *piazza* on the site of an amphitheatre. Small shops and restaurants are everywhere. The architecture is stunning wherever you look. It must have been hard to decide on which of the two immense churches to confer the *Duomo*-ship. There are museums, an art gallery, there is even an opera house. One of the many *piazze* is large enough to act as an open-air arena for all kinds of entertainment. Armida and I attended an Elton John concert – one talented little chap at a piano performing non-stop on his own for close on three hours. Captivating stuff. The place was packed and the crowd enraptured.

Behind the temporary stage and occupying the length of that side of the square is the Palazzo Ducale which was undergoing a

Lucca

facelift. It had been screened off by a huge bleached and sized calico curtain hanging from roof level down to the ground. On it frames had been painted to match the style and position of the actual window openings, I should think some sixty or seventy of them. Local artists were then invited to fill the spaces with their own work. It was a huge success. Some had chosen to paint pastiches of well-known paintings; others had gone for a humorous approach. One I recollect particularly. A man and woman could be seen talking at an "open" sash window. Depicted hanging outside from the ledge on a knotted sheet was the trouserless figure of a man. I have wondered recently whether Banksy was in the crowd poaching ideas.

Florence from
Santo Miniato
al Monte

§   §   §

We have strayed from the eating-out theme so may I now steer us back and to Florence in case you are ever in need of a good and affordable place to eat in this expensive city. Here is one of my favourites that should fit the description and goes by the appealing as well as pronounceable name of Il Pandemonio. It is on the via del Leone near the Piazza Torquato Tasso, the end further from the Arno. The atmosphere is amazing, the clientele international. It is to be hoped that the owners, husband and wife, still run the place. He is head chef, she the principal *cameriera*, her height perfect for looking the seated diners straight in the eye. The wines could be very expensive but one was paying for the experience as well as the food. I confidently brought visitors here for gourmet meals but one is really spoiled for choice in this *quartiere*.

It was in Florence that I had my pocket picked. The Velottis were on holiday so I had been able to drive in to the centre mid-week to do some personal shopping. I parked near the *stazione* – you can tell how well I'm getting on with the vocabulary – and headed for the river

The Butler Did It

and the Uffizi gallery. A family (I didn't think of them as a gang until later) of seven or so gypsy children, probably Albanian, were being shepherded along by the eldest, a girl of about 15 no more, pushing a pram. I smiled as I drew near and they smiled back as we jostled past each other on the narrow pavement. I decided to make for the Piazza della Repubblica for a cappuccino (that's the same in Italian) and strode on. I hadn't gone very far when one of them, a small boy I'd particularly noticed with the cheekiest of faces, stopped me and handed me my wallet. *"Scusate, Signor"* he said looking tearful. I hadn't even noticed it had gone. He waited while I checked inside; nothing had been taken. I wondered if these gypsies had mistaken me for a cleric – I was dressed as usual, completely in black; plus, I have been told, I do exude an irritatingly pious aura a lot of the time, though most especially in repose. Perhaps this urchin had been scolded by his superstitious sister for stealing from a holy man and risking bad luck upon them. So, thinking quickly, I gave him a blessing. [Well, I had the Latin, you see; useful at last.] *"Grazie"*, he said, cheered up and ran off. Quite an encounter.

I went straight to the nearest gentlemen's outfitters and spent all the money I had on shirts and shoes before a more hardened gang of thieves could get their nimble fingers on it. I also made a mental note to make a habit of wearing my uniform when walking in Italian cities.

Later, I noticed my comb was missing; it had been in the same pocket. A pity, that. We had covered a considerable mileage together since I bought it in Japan and it achieved a fame of sorts in Westbury Meets East as a comb *with instructions.*

§ § §

When it came to my annual holiday in 1999 I booked, with help from Anna, the recently appointed secretary, a young Englishwoman who spoke perfect Italian, a week in Sicily followed by a week based on Lipari in the Aeolian Islands.

It was May and already in the 30s Celsius when I landed at Catania and joined a cosmopolitan group of jolly tourists on a coach tour. Led by Salvatore our genial guide, philosopher and friend who proved to be a gem (knowledgeable, amusing and *simpatico*), we travelled the well-worn route, judging by all the other buses parked up next to ours at every stop, starting with Taormina then Céfalu, Palermo, Monreale, Trapani, Marsala, Selinunte, Agrigento and Siracusa (ruins, mosaics, amphitheatres, traditional dancing and more ruins – more here than in Greece it is claimed and probably true; I've no plans to go and check). Back at Catania we wished each other "Adios!", "Au revoir!", "Sayonara!", "Bye-bye!" or "Seeya!" and "Addio!" to Salvatore.

Palermo

Selinunte

Céfalu

I missed the connection with the local bus.

It had been hiding behind a hoarding in the airport car park. I can still see myself in slow motion – partly because I couldn't run any faster with my heavy suitcase – waving and shouting as the bus pulled away gathering speed to the sound of laughter from the crowd. So it meant a taxi to Milazzo for the crossing over to Lipari.

The pretty winding route chosen by the driver and significantly more to his financial advantage than the direct one took us close to Mount Etna. At that time a period of unusually intense activity had endured for a considerable while; without producing an eruption. Now it is well-known that the Italians and the Sicilians share a mutual dislike. [This fact is put to clever use: a huge percentage of the Italian *Corpo di Polizia* is recruited in Sicily.] I remember earlier in the year noticing on the harbour wall at Livorno, where the ferry leaves for Palermo, the *graffito* that translates as "Come On Etna – You Can Do It!"

The drive was sufficiently exciting in itself – take a look at the map – but I did make it in time to be the last foot passenger to board the final ferry of the evening.

§ § §

With a thirst to see as many of the islands as possible I'm afraid I rather ignored Lipari itself. I only strayed from the port area once to hurriedly purchase a beach towel to take on the first day-trip, it being explained that the boat would moor in one of the bays so those passengers who wished could take a swim. How was I to know that, apart from the skipper, I was to be the only male on the outing? Oh never mind; we're off now.

I estimate that there must have been approaching thirty ladies on board, all speaking in German. When the boat eventually sailed into this bay and dropped anchor, none of them moved; all eyes were on me. In fact a chant started up. I didn't need to know the words – it was clear they were waiting for me to strip off and jump in. Well I already had my trunks on under my shorts and it would be a shame not to use the towel bought especially. A whoop went up when I jumped in and the deck rail was soon lined with these grinning faces *and* their cameras. Well I have always been one to pander to the

The Butler Did It

ladies and I began to perform some stunts. It was strange that none of *them* had been keen to swim and I wondered why they weren't actually taking photos.

They had seen what I hadn't seen. The reason for their encouragement *and* all the cameras was because a huge shoal of *medusa* were swimming closer and closer to me, waving their poisonous stinging tentacles and promising some entertainment! If the *capitano* hadn't seen what was going on and thrown me down a rope ladder the air would have been filled with the laughter of a lot of raucous, cackling, camera-clicking *Frauen*. A narrow escape.

The boat set off again for Stromboli, famous for its volcano of course; but also for Roberto Rossellini's film featuring Ingrid Bergman his leading lady and bedmate at the time; and the fine black volcanic lava beaches which somehow don't look right at all. Plus there's the fact that nowadays Dolce & Gabbano the style gurus have a villa here. It had been a bit of a haul and was almost dark before the boat docked.

The neighbouring isle of Salina was also worth the visit and much, much nearer. Its twin volcanoes help to identify it from the others but it's not a competition that I would win; it seems to me it all depends on your direction of approach. It is where the Malvasia grape is grown with which they make a remarkably good dessert wine. If you're a film buff you would already know that the 1995 film 'Il Postino' was made here.

As for the remaining islands, I made the acquaintance of a French lady staying at the same hotel and we didn't manage to reach any more but I'm pretty sure that as well as being beautiful they all have black lava sand beaches and have been the setting for an award-winning film or two in the past. She and I had a few days to concentrate on the present.

§ § §

The Italian Job

Deceptive calm of the bay

Holidays *can* be unsettling but those two weeks away from the workplace had restored my equilibrium for want of a better name to give it and confirmed my suspicion that it was the lack of female company that had been making me a dull boy. Encounters with the opposite sex since my arrival in Tuscany had been limited to flirting with the check-out girls at the *supermercato* (and I must say, when it comes to talent, the Esselunga here wins easily over the Sainsbury's back in Wiltshire) or with the two very attractive and really helpful ladies who ran the *Agenzia Postale* and to whom I gave perfume at Christmas. One was exceptionally pretty and the other you'd describe as handsome but I never got to know them well enough to be able to determine their polarity, so to speak. Then there was the pedicurist

Farewell to the Aeolian Islands

The Butler Did It

with the exquisite pair and the lovely Norwegian physio/masseuse, Ingelise, with whom I maintained a professional contact after she had helped my brother with his dodgy back. This was the extent of my integration with the locals. Further afield in Pescia, I stumbled on a Club Cabaret called Kan Dariya in the Piazza Mercato that was open on Sunday evenings. I went in and sat with a glass of Italian fizz to watch the dancing but the atmosphere had none of the charm of Shirakawa's Makati Club. My beautiful Russian table companion begged me to stay but only, I think, to practise her English. I left without finishing my drink.

Printed on a local supermarket plastic bag for the benefit of English shoppers:

> HERE, WE BEG, DON'T ABANDON IT IN THE ENVIRONMENT BUT
> OF USE IT MORE TIMES FOR THE TRANSPORT OF GOODS AND,
> SUBSEQUENTLY, FOR THE HANDLING OF THE DOMESTIC REFUSALS

Oh, if only more of us could learn to handle the domestic refusals.

Purely in the interests of bonding, I invited Anna and Armida one Sunday, while the Velottis were away, to lunch with me on the covered terrace above the library. To make the fourth, I asked Camilla if she'd like to join us, a Swedish girl who came to wait at table from time to time when the occasion and the guest numbers warranted the extra help. She lived a short walk away. [Someone at the Villa, I tactfully forget who it was, once described her Italian accent as like "that of a Pisan *puttana.*"]

After an initial awkwardness I think it went quite well. Anna helped with the language hurdle. They seemed surprised I'd gone to so much trouble and Anna melted a bit. The feeling when they left was very much that we should do it again.

It was well into the summer before the Velottis went off on their travels again. My Sundays were very precious to me especially when I had the place to myself and could completely relax simply by staying put and enjoying the glorious weather and very privately situated pool. One day I decided to ask Camilla if she'd like to come on Sunday for a swim. She was delighted.

When she arrived she wasn't carrying anything so I assumed she had her swimming things on underneath. Not at all. She wasn't the least bit shy.

The secluded pool.

The Italian Job

She just stripped off and jumped in. And that's how the afternoon passed; we swam and we splashed. She had a discreet rose tattoo on her right shoulder and another tastefully positioned in the centre of her perfectly formed left buttock and I didn't care what her voice sounded like because we didn't talk a lot. The butler served the wine and the waitress served her purpose. I suppose things would have worked out differently if the others had turned up but they weren't going to turn up because they hadn't been invited.

§ § §

A rare diary entry from October 1999.

A chance to scribble a few lines. I've been working in Italy for roughly a year now and I'm able to say more than "La Cena é servita." Summer is changing into autumn and I'm sitting at a table in the Piazza Santo Spirito. I've ordered my lunch and while waiting for it to be served by the prettiest of the waitresses - I should think she's what one of the American comedians call a "suicide blonde" (dyed by her own hand) - I am sipping a glass of rosso and reflecting on my general good luck. This house wine looks thin but drinks strong. There is time to walk it off before driving back to Lucca. I plan to take a stroll later in the Boboli Gardens, recommended by my daughters who came to stay last week, pronouncing them Bobbly. Thinking about it is making me giggle. Here comes the waitress; very nice.

Later. I've just enjoyed the most ginormous plate of spigola (sea-bass, salad, etc.). It's fun when eating out alone to tune into nearby conversations while pretending to read the giornale and there are the visual delights, too, resulting from the lowered eye-level and enhanced by the effect of the wine as new arrivals brush by the table. I'm wondering if I'll make it to the Bobbly Gardens this time. Everyone is so friendly here; I feel disinclined to budge.

Much later still. Interesting girl, Sabrina (the waitress) - I got to know a lot about her, including the fact that she's not a natural blonde and I didn't have to ask her. It was just uncovered in the course of the evening. The gardens will still be there when I come back next week and so will she.

§ § §

As the days became shorter the frequency of entertaining at the Villa increased and we enjoyed a succession of evenings with famous names in the film, television and theatre world. But those I preferred by far were when Signor Velotti's old university chums and their other halves were invited with whom I could usually share a joke. It was getting towards the end of the year and during such a dinner party that one of the bunch asked me about my holiday. How did it go? I thanked him for asking and gave a short reply but that didn't seem enough. Perhaps he had noticed the twinkle in my eye and he pressed me for details. So, in Italian, I told them about the boat trip when I found myself with about thirty other passengers, ALL women; and I grinned. They laughed. Pause. *"Tutte tedesci!"* (ALL GERMANS!) raised my eyebrows and looked resigned. They chuckled. Pause. *"Piu di ottanta!"* (OVER 80 YEARS OLD!) and looked totally peeved. They roared. I think this might have been my undoing because it got the largest laugh of the evening. The Dottore was used to being the centre of attention with his jokes and anecdotes and the butler had unintentionally upstaged him. Oh lor'.

§ § §

The last hours of the old year and the first few of the Millenium were spent in the Buca di Sant'Antonio. My boss and his wife had very thoughtfully included me in the landmark celebrations and I found myself sitting at the same table with all the house-guests. Signora Velotti placed me next to her, anticipating perhaps that I might have felt uncomfortable having been a servant to them all for the previous few days. Well it was better than leaving me outside in the car and I could be relied upon to use the correct cutlery.

At 3 a.m. on the 1st January 2000, I was on the point of turning off my bedside lamp when I thought of my father. Born in April 1900, will he make it to his century?

§ § §

The news of my father was not very good and I began to think of returning to England to join other members of the family who were already providing support to my mother. In February, I began packing up my non-essential belongings and delivering them unobtrusively to the local shipper for storage until I was ready.

Towards the end of the month I had decided to give notice to the Velottis of my imminent departure. At lunch one day the Signora asked me to come and see her in the kitchen when I'd finished tidying up. There she told me that the house would be in chaos for a number of months while the dining-room was being extended and major structural alterations would be taking place. My services would not be required or even possible. She then apologised for the short notice but could I please move out within a few days. It was not difficult to act dismayed Where would I go with such little warning? *She* had it all worked out. Surely I could go and stay with my brother until the tenant moved out of my cottage in Wiltshire. I did my best to look appalled. Fifteen minutes later and it would have been *me* handing in my notice.

The way things stood, the Velottis were now obliged to pay my air fare home. They were not too happy about that but they didn't make too much fuss and a *surprisingly* few days later I was ready to be driven byArmida to Pisa's Galileo Galilei Airport.

§ § §

2nd March 2000; airborne, Pisa to Stansted.

Thinking of becoming a butler? It's an equal opportunity these days, ladies. Sir Alec Guinness was quoted as saying that "actors were awarded knighthoods so that they could become butlers." It's true, some acting experience could be very useful. Some hold the opinion that "butlers rule the world". Maybe some do, but we'll never know because humility is paramount. It's in the rules.

So what do you need? Well, a flair for anticipating trouble and handling u-turns; then a natural diplomacy would be useful and on top of that the ability to balance the books. All the qualities that are lacking in our politicians. Plus a good sense of humour and the ability to laugh at yourself without anyone hearing. Remember the rule about the furniture.

So, I wish you the huge amount of luck that's come my way and much less silver to polish.

Oh, just a minute. Look down there. That's the Baron's pad; I wonder if they've finished stripping the wallpaper.

§ § §

On the 11th April 2000 my father made it to 100. You'd have liked him. Everybody did. He died on the 7th November. R.I.P.

§ § §

There must have been something going on in his subconscious whilst airborne back to Blighty because the Italian job turned out to be Westbury's last. The uniforms – daytime, evening and ceremonial – were bagged up and stowed in a wardrobe. They eventually saw the light of day again for book-signings and after-dinner speaking; and as we shall see in Part Two...family weddings.

The Butler Did It

Westbury Heads South – Part Two

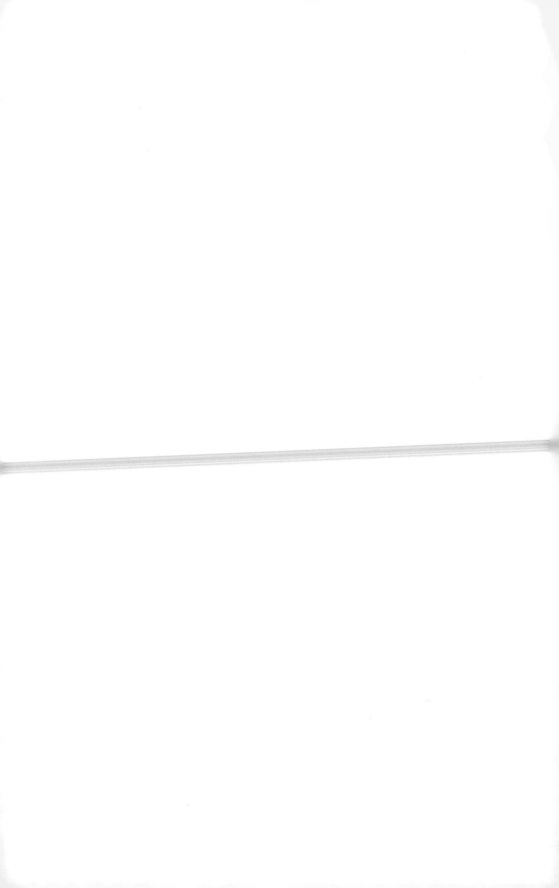

Introduction

WITH THE ODDS AGAINST HIM, *the month of September 2000 saw Westbury motoring through strike-torn France in search of somewhere to live. After a journey zig-zagging across the Corrèze, Lot, Aveyron, Lozère, Gard, Hérault and Tarn departments, his diary reads:*

29th September. A shinkansen it is not but this stopping train from Dreux to Montparnasse is a very smart double-decker affair that normally speeds like an arrow between stations and through some beautiful scenery including the fringes of the Forêt de Rambouillet. Normalement. Not today. The SNCF workers are on a go-slow which is why at 10a.m. nothing is moving and I am using this pause to reflect on my travels of the last five weeks which were complicated by the strike of the lorry drivers refusing to deliver petrol. Who'd want to go and live in damp Socialist France? Concentrating my search south-west of a line from Limoges to Avignon, I've settled for the cliché of a place in the Dordogne, the Périgord Noir, to be more precise. It is a property sans running water, sans electricity, sans everything; but avec an outstanding view. I intend to transform this abandoned sheep farm into a home.

I've left the car today with some Twinning friends at Houdan in order to spend some time in Paris. I'm on my own this time and the plan is to locate the hotel particulier in the rue de Grenelle in the hope that Venezia is home, the Franco-Polish fashion model I met in Fukushima. Hello - we're on the move again.

§ § §

On the 28ᵗʰ of February 2001 I crossed by channel ferry from Dover to Calais. The very bored douanier took his time turning the pages of my passport.

Lui: Vous avez beaucoup voyagé, M'sieur.

Moi : Oui, on pourrait dire ça.

Lui : Japon…Malaisie…les Philippines…Nouvelle Zélande… Nouvelle Calédonie ! Que faites-vous comme métier ?

Moi : Je suis retraité.

Lui : (avec impatience) Ouais ! Mais avant !

[At that time I didn't know the French for 'butler' so I chose one aspect of the job that would do to answer his question.]
Moi: J'étais sommelier.
[There was a pause.]
Lui: Un sommelier ANGLAIS !!?

WELCOME TO FRANCE

Chapter One
La France Profonde I

Episode One: Getting Connected

MARCH. I ARRIVED TO FIND that my instructions regarding water and electricity had been ignored. José, the brother of the vendor, was unsurprised. "C'est normal! EDF? C'est un grand bordel!" Fortunately for me he had already come to the rescue and the caravan *d'occasion*, which had been delivered on time, was now moored (there's been a lot of rain) for the time being in the courtyard of his farm on the other side of the lane and connected up to his water and electricity. Good man. Let's get cracking.

§ § §

A few days later, on my return from the Crédit Agricole, the farmers' bank, where I'd received lots of free advice regarding, for example, changing the number plates on my car to French ones (the French government, struggling to win favour with the voters, has put an end to motor tax), I found an electrician abseiling down a concrete post to instal a *compteur de chantier* which will be valid for one year while I make at least a part of the old *bergerie* habitable. One year may be optimistic – we'll see. So that's the electricity fixed up, what's happening about the water supply? Tenants are due to move into José's farm soon and they won't want to find my caravan blocking their entrance.

A team from the Compagnie des Eaux et l'Ozone arrived on the 18th – three trucks plus a trailer with a JCB – and set about locating the mains pipe. They'd been issued with no plan and there wasn't a hazel twig between them. As they dug, a long deep narrow ditch grew in the field opposite heading for the horizon…

The next day two men turned up at about 11.30, dug a short trench from the corner of the barn to the edge of the lane and went to lunch. When I saw them again they were happily playing with something called a *taupe* (mole). This is in the shape of a small torpedo with a vibrating nozzle and like a mole it tunnels underground. Powered by a generator through a long flexible tube attached at the back, it was lowered into the trench over on the field side. Tck, tck, tck. I'd asked for minimum nuisance to the local traffic and this was what they'd come up with. Great. How long did they think it would take? A shrug, then *"Une heure ou deux. Normalement."*

When I returned expectantly from La Poste half an hour later, I was dismayed to see glum faces. Bernard, the elder of the two who rolls his own Gauloise Leger *sèches*, was kitted out in spotless yellow overalls when I left. Now he was mud-*coloured* from the waist down and mud-*spattered* from the waist up including his spectacles. *"Avez-vous eu de succès?"* I enquired. I could see him counting up to *dix*. A characteristic that the mechanical gadget shares with the real live creature is that it is short-sighted. "We have a problem", he said with a half-smile. "The mole's *lunettes* were broken last week and while they are in the workshop for *réparation* we have to try to manage without. *Malheureusement* we cannot tell whether she is going to the left or right. Now we shall try from the opposite direction."

They also fished around in their kit and found a metal detector which showed that directionally things now seemed to be going well, although the signal got gradually weaker. I didn't like to say anything – you don't do you – but it was clear that while the mole *was* making steady forward progress she was also going *deeper*! By the time she'd completed the programmed distance she'd fallen short of the target area.

Further determined excavation by JCB and shovel (it was beginning to get dark) resulted in more slapstick, there being no shortage of the requisite ingredients, mud and water. They were absolutely coated to the point where they could only be distinguished from one another by Yves' beret. They promised me they'd take a shower before going to bed.

Messrs. Grin & Beret were back in the morning to complete the *embranchement*.

§ § §

Following the episode of *"La taupe qui fait comme elle veut"* [in the vein of *"La vache qui rit, etc."*], the constant rain showed up the high level of the water-table and so, what with the presence of clay, when the time came for the telephone connection I settled for an overhead cable and a wooden post and no burrowing underground. Nobody else seems the least bit concerned about 'The Look' of the place. Dotted all over this lovely countryside is a jumble of poles made of concrete or wood or zinc carrying cables of every sort, some of which are touching the ground as a result of high winds. Nobody cares. *"C'est la campagne!"*, they say. Looking around I sometimes think I've come to live in a Third World country – which, I'm surprising myself

The Butler Did It

by writing, really shouldn't displease me to the point of criticism as everything adds up to the rural charm of where I have come to live: no motorway noise, distant views to the Auvergne, not a pylon to be seen.

Towards the end of the month, I returned from a shopping trip to find, *sooner* than expected, a lorry full of gravel parked at the top near the barn but no sign of anybody. My excitement subsided and I got on with the day's business: boundary fencing. At about 11a.m. there was the sound of an approaching engine which slowed, slightly, then made a dramatic entrance accelerating through the new opening and on to the property. 10 metres further and the JCB was axle deep in mud. That is quite deep. The following 30 minutes was spent levering, reversing, tearing out of hair, gnashing of teeth – all to no benefit except that I learned a few more French colloquialisms. It had been agreed with the contractor that because the terrain was not in a stable enough state, gravel would first have to be spread on a layer of fibreglass matting before any heavy vehicles could be used. So the ground-worker, Claude to his friends, Clod to me, had not got off to a good start. The place for the hole to be dug for the *fosse septique* was still some distance down the slope so he'd better concentrate on recovering his composure, extricating the JCB more scientifically and building the entry road . My benefactor, José, having

Third World or "rural charm"?

heard the cursing, came over for a word and in the few minutes that I was distracted Clod had backed up his gravel-laden truck across the *chemin* D62E3 and straight into the trench only recently filled in by the chaps from the Water Board. Now it was the lorry that was axle-deep in the mud; except that they use a different word for mud round here. You hear it quite a lot. This is not what you'd call a busy lane but, once a lorry is stuck across it, it is amazing what a build-up of spectators it can create in no time at all. And everyone had an opinion as to what the poor man should do. It was actually the *facteur* on his rounds in his yellow van who finally drove the truck free from the sucking mud while Clod applied his recently acquired skills of leverage, reversing, tearing of hair and gnashing of teeth and the whole site finally reverted to how it was. He *said* he will be back on Monday. *Normalement.* Probably for more of the same.

The weather remained dreadful and another week passed before I saw Claude again. Conditions were now more favourable and over the next five days the landscape was transformed to give me enough flat area for a terrace, the position for the *épandage* decided and pegged out, the hole dug and the septic tank in the ground and prepared for final connection on the Monday. Great. It looked as though after days of trench warfare it was all going to happen.

Saturday. The overnight storm, which was forecast, had brought a freshness to the morning as I descended the hillside in excellent mood. Until, that is, I rounded the corner of the farmhouse. The amount of rain had set adrift 1500 kilograms of concrete septic tank which was now listing to starboard. Dislodged pipes and joints and hoses and clips were now mere flotsam bumping against its sides like débris round a shipwreck. *"La fosse septique qui flotte!"*

Yesterday, settled in its rightful place it was a symbol of triumph, evidence of achievement at last. Today, I am pleased to be alone as there is no-one to witness my frustration, *'ni la catastrophe, ni les larmes'*. Surely he should have done some strategic back-filling of earth or part-filling the tank with water to weigh it down. But I'm sure the contractor's excuse will start with: *"Normalement..."*

§ § §

Tales of the unexpected could fill many more pages of this memoir. For example, in the process of demolishing a flight of stone steps a nest of snakes was exposed. They escaped into the undergrowth; better there than in close proximity to what would become the guest bedroom. Then there was the mishap of the end-wall that collapsed. One day it was there and the next it wasn't. The contractor acted very quickly, marshalled a team of men and by the end of the morning 26 acrow props were in place and a new concrete floor was being poured.

§ § §

In brief, it took nearly four years for Westbury to make enough of the place fit for occupation and for him to move out of the caravan. Along the way he stumbled into plenty of linguistic traps, the so-called 'faux amis' There are no "bons viveurs' in France – they are 'bons vivants'; you cannot be guilty of a 'double entendre' but you can of a 'double entente'; and if you refer to a womaniser as an old 'roué', they do not know what you are talking about – they come straight out with it – he is a 'séducteur'. If something is awful (the weather, the taste, a work of art), 'ce n'est pas terrible' meaning it is

The Butler Did It

not just terrible, it's worse than terrible! But the English are just as bad: how can anything be awfully good?

§ § §

When he wasn't engaged in what he began to think of as his life's work, he found relaxation, when the muse obliged, in writing about the French way of life as he saw it; and other stuff. Sometimes it took the form of essays or reviews or just accounts of bizarre events that happened. And with easy access to the whole of Europe he began again to do some travelling. It is hoped that you find what follows entertaining. But if you are looking for someone to blame…the secret's in the title: The Butler Did It.

Episode Two : Settling In

The natives seemed friendly and why shouldn't they be. In keeping with French law, the local farmers had been given first refusal on the land. As the steep slope made it unsuitable for anything other than sheep-grazing, there were no takers and the abandoned building was not habitable. Built in the 1850s it had been added to twice; to accommodate sheep at one end and cattle at the other. The last human occupant was a widowed shepherdess who had died nearly 40 years ago and the place had been empty ever since. There was also a detached barn up near the entrance from the lane. It had only three

The Slope

walls and a rusting iron roof but it gave the caravan useful protection from the prevailing wind.

I learned most of the local history from my nearest neighbours a 5-minute walk away when I knocked on their door just to introduce myself. I'd been warned not to get too *close* to the locals and that what they say to your face may differ to that when your back is turned. It is a regional characteristic, apparently, for which there is a phrase -*'faux cul'*- which is rather crude (but not as rude as the phonetically similar phrase in English). It means 'hypocrytical'.

I also found out that I'm living in *'les picadis'*, the Périgordine equivalent of 'the sticks' and that 'Chanteranne' (part of my address) means 'song of the frogs', whose duck impersonations I can hear most evenings from the lake below.

As time passes I've become aware of the undercurrents. No – not in the lake but among

the neighbours (*les riverains*). It is very noticeable that some are not speaking to each other and they do not all attend the village events in the *salle des fêtes*. This is huntin' and shootin' country (no horses, just guns and dogs) and fatalities have occurred in recent times; gossip has it that they may not have been accidental. Family feuds are rife, dating probably from wartime collaboration with the enemy which is well documented in this region. Best not to go there. Not far from here there is a tiny hamlet of three families where none of them communicate with each other; so it is said. I talk to anyone and everybody; it helps to practice my French.

⌈There is just a handful of ex-pats in these parts; which is manageable. There are some towns where, on market days, you hear *only* English voices. All the year round!⌉

§   §   §

The need for body repairs and maintenance has widened my French vocabulary and brought me into contact with some charming ladies of various disciplines. "*Les dames qui s'occupe de mon corps.*"

It is the season of *le rhume des foins* (hay fever) and I'm keeping an appointment with the *infirmière* to obtain a jab. I roll up my sleeve but she wags her finger. A lot can be achieved with mime in these early days. She wants me *sans culottes*. More mime. "*Vive la Révolution!*" I say out loud. She smiles and insists "*C'est normal!*"; she wants to get at *mes fesses* (my buttocks). ⌈She's not the first; though not widely publicised, they won 'Best in Berkshire' awards in their hey-day.⌉ So, when in France…do as the French. I drop my trousers. She smiles again, pinches the left one and gently in goes the needle. It'll be four weeks before I can have another injection. I'll be counting the days.

Here's a test for you. *Ma dentiste, elle est très jolie, très mignonne, très parfumée, très proche…et très professionnelle…hélas.* I feel quite well acquainted with the lady after a series of investigative probes. There is a very good chance that she has saved a tooth now that she has found the root cause. She has a caring manner, speaks softly and to be so close is most distracting.

Ma coiffeuse is a young lady with the prettiest of faces and a definite comeliness about everything below. She takes a bit of flirting in her stride and I prefer to call in person to make an appointment instead of telephoning. There are usually some *dames d'un certain âge* in the middle of some curious beautification ritual involving lotions and ironmongery. I'm aware of their eyes following my every move. Well that's the whole point, really. Of course I have to make my apology to each of them in person for having interrupted the *processus important*. This is so that they and I get the chance for a close-up. I know that I can rely on Christèle to let them know I'm single but so far there's not been one to *chatouiller mon ardeur*.

Ma dermatologue is stay-alive gorgeous. I'm seeing her for my *cuir cheval*, just so you know. "Queer what?" I hear you cry. Nothing rude, it's just my scalp and there's nothing quite like her touch with a head massage.

And lastly, *ma Kinésithérapeute*. She is very popular with the men. She has us all in the palm of her hand.

Episode Three – Une soirée mémorable!

The trick with invitations, I find, is to do your best to see them coming and have an excuse lined up. I had heard on the *téléphone arabe* (French for grapevine, would you believe!) that there is a yearly fixture – *Le Repas de Chasse* (the Hunters' Lunch) – that (as it was described by my informant) "tests to the full the organisational and culinary resources of two neighbouring *communes* : Saint Hyroïde la Glande and La Chabellerie". It didn't sound much like my sort of thing.

On this occasion I was taken offguard by the friendly direction whence the invitation came. Jerry Myers, a not overtly joyful soul – but a near neighbour and upright citizen of St Hyroïde nevertheless, who had, hitherto at any rate, always seemed well-disposed towards me – pre-empted my instinctive resistance and lack of enthusiasm for the event by informing me, with what sounded very much like pride, that he had only failed to attend the raypah once since moving here, with Margot his wife, six years ago. That was last year when he was laid low by *La Grippe*. His tone of voice implied that here was something not to be missed. It was only afterwards that I learned – too late to be taken into my reckoning – of Margot's annual abstention after only one experience.

Actually, I had a number of perfectly legitimate reasons for declining, including a last minute resurgence of toothache. However, surely I could rely on the good-natured, unbiased recommendation of a fellow-countryman. *Normalement, oui.*

Well I found out the hard way. Jerry's pride in respect of his inexplicable record of attendance must be something he measures in masochistic units of endurance, starting with trial by accordion, a fiendish device that hit us like an acoustic stun-gun the second we were inside the door. The occupant of the instrument ("maestro" did not apply) – who had been engaged *professionally*, mind (let us be clear: he was being paid) – eventually raised the spirits of an increasingly hungry and impatient throng composed of fifty to sixty people, glassy-eyed and incredulous, drawn together through a set of circumstances ranging from duty, to being in the wrong place at the wrong time, by rewarding them with a break in his musical battles as well as those of his short wide be-sequinned orange-dyed balding songstress of a wife.

Respite was, however, short-lived as there was – "Oh *no!*" – a surprise in store in the shape of a reserve back-up of willing amateurs in the wings queueing up to be strapped into the bellows during the interval. So the cacophony continued relentlessly. Let me not be guilty of exaggeration. Torture is an emotive word so let me moderate my language and explain in measured tones that any control that *might* have been exercised over the amplifiers up to this point now yielded to an increase in conversation-defying decibels of a piercing magnitude that assumed new levels of audio-sadism as the amateurs now ran amok with the electrical equipment. The *Salle des Fêtes* was about to melt.

Just as heads were on the point of splitting, a rescue operation of sorts was mounted. Purple ink, included in the meal ticket, was dispensed from unlabelled wine-bottles and quickly brought about a welcome numbness, for which they, the management, could have actually named their price.

Two seriously dedicated senior citizens, mother and daughter, provided a distraction, twirling robotically in ever-decreasing circles at high tempo, one-two-three, one-two-three, sufficient to make the on-lookers giddy. Soon there was a feeling of "Hey, we're all in this together" and "Seeing as we're here anyway" so that, before long, helped by copious quantities of the low-grade wine [remember: this is the land with the *savoir-faire* to produce *and export* huge amounts of its unwanted Beaujolais Nouveau], what with the smoke, the cooking fumes and the condensation there was an atmosphere that nearly passed for *ambiance*. The place was jumping.

The food, when it came, was unspeakable. It was just as well that the steam veiled the cooking methods in the miniscule partitioned-off scullery next to the way in, where an obscene abundance of very

The Butler Did It

identifiable animal-parts were over-cooked and under-cooked at random by two or three volunteers (no room for more) who, it was noticed, did not actually participate in the feast. Thanks in particular to the soup, a broth of sorts containing flotsam of uncertain origin but chiefly chunks of bread well-submerged among the butter beans, the walk home was likely to be a good deal quicker than the walk there. [At first I did well with Périgordine cooking; that was before I made the mistake of translating the ingredients.] A local delicacy followed the soup: gizzard salad. Next, roe-deer parts marinaded in vintage BR Brown Windsor gravy. Then roast venison with sliced potatoes, onions and garlic (to distinguish it from the roe-deer). Camembert served with lots of bread. Finally a selection of home-made desserts that had been arriving with the guests: apple charlottes, sultana cheesecake, flans and something that looked like apple pizza. Coffee was served once the Baccarat beakers were emptied and topped up with some lethal liquid, 58° proof and probably illegally distilled. Man cannot live by bread alone...so I majored on the apple charlottes. We had each of us paid €14 for the privilege. [About £8.90 at the time.]

We listened to what was last year's "Thank you" speech (I was told) by this year's Social Committee Chairman in which attention was drawn to the most expensive food item: the potatoes! The same recipes, the same jokes, I supposed. *Plus ça change, plus c'est la même chose.* The butter beans were a gift from a farmer with a glut; *and* a terrible stoop which became evident when he stood up to acknowledge the applause. From the look of the meat, the hunters had kept the best for themselves.

As for my neighbour Jerry, the devil won a bottle of Ricard in the tombola, thereby breaking even. The rest of us will just have to put it down to experience.

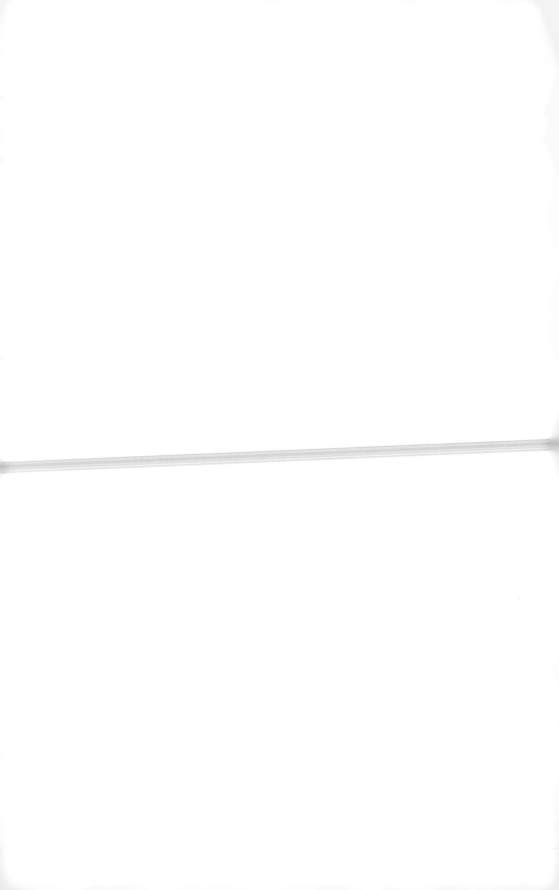

Chapter Two
Three Weddings...

THREE FAMILY WEDDINGS OCCURRED WITHIN a few months of each other. The first saw me in Stockholm where my nephew was to marry his Swedish bride. They very flatteringly dug me out of retirement to perform toastmaster duties at the reception. In turn, I dug my white-tie-and-tails out of the wardrobe and flew over in good time to meet the toast*mistress* and to discuss the programme. We put our heads together, her pretty one and mine, to come up with some ideas to take into account the Anglo-Swedish flavour of the occasion.

To involve *all* the guests and solve the language difference I suggested adopting the Victorian Music Hall tradition of audience participation aided by the recording-studio technique of so-called 'idiot cards'. I would take on the rôle of Chairman, of course. The idea of the 'accident' with the sari, to expose her lovely fishnet-tight encased legs, was entirely Mica's – it had to be – it couldn't *possibly* have come from me. We drafted a bit of a script to use as link material between the customary entertainment from the guests (it is usual for there to be anything up to twenty speeches or songs or readings at a Swedish wedding) and made some appropriately worded cards:

HEAR, HEAR!	SHAME!	Oh no he ISN'T!

AT ENORMOUS EXPENSE!	Ooooooh!

Aaaaaah!	Poor old Girl!	NEVER!

§ § §

The theme was "Peas"! As in: "As alike as Two Peas in a Pod!" The programme, the place-cards, etc. were all printed accordingly. They want peas, I'll give them P's, I thought. So, in true flamboyant Leonard Sachs style:

"*BRIDE & GROOM, Laydees & Gentlemen, Proud Parents and Pulchritudinous Participants,*

"*Let peas predominate! Please prepare yourselves for the programme proper, a plethora, nay a pot-pourri of pertinent out-pourings, penetrating in their perspicacity, provocative in their pasquinade, painstaking in their presentation but never [NEVER!] pedantic in their performance.*

"*Pitchforked into paradoxical prominence by their own peremptory pontificating, the pavonine protagonists will playfully propound their peculiar patronising patter primed by personal prejudice to promulgate the peccadilloes of our prince and his princess [Aaaaaah!]. Pin back your pinnae for the palpably palatable, the positively pleasurable and the potentially psychedelic (the "p" is silent as in "bath")*

"*Persevere with the pathetic, prescind the prolonged, praise the perfunctory and pity the perfectly paralytic. [Ooooooh!] . A plague on all proponents of pernicious or pragmatic propaganda. If, peradventure, people persist in the pursuit of pretentiously punctuated parameters producing a panoply of protest, I propose to pre-empt the pain in the proverbial by plugging with paracetemol or promoting the provision of prunes! [HEAR, HEAR!] A pox on puritanical platitudes and enough preposterous prattle from this pulpit. By way of parenthesis and provided I remain perpendicular, I shall prevail on all pilgrims who are perceived to have peregrinated from*

peripheral parts [AT ENORMOUS EXPENSE!] *not to claim privilege in the perpetration of puns. They will be passionately penalised.*

"Here endeth the Prologue. [MORE!!] *Perish the possibility! And so to the proceedings proper."*

[In the event of hecklers: *"Pelargoniums and potash to you, sir!"* or *"Permanganate of potassium!"* or *"Prettily put!".*]

[*Westbury would love you to think that he delivered all this by heart. He didn't.*]

Later in the proceedings I announced *"A turn for the worst! For your delectation and delight we have combined two favourite features of the English stage: Olde Time Music Hall and the Pantomime Dame. Specially flown in from the Players' Theatre, London* [AT ENORMOUS EXPENSE!] *to lead you in her famous rendering of "Why am I always the Bridesmaid?" – Please welcome: Miss Patsy Rowlands."*

To make this work I had sought the help of two volunteers. As we were leaving the church, I asked Johan and Anton whether they would be willing to help me in a performance. When they heard they would be required to wear women's clothing, they didn't hesitate. At some opportune moment backstage, I grabbed them for a quick run-through of 'The Bridesmaid's Lament', handing them each a dress, a wig and a lipstick. They really did me proud. The next time I saw them they had transformed themselves into big-bosomed ugly sisters.

I had no option but to make my own transformation in full view with Mica's help.

"Now Ladies and Gentlemen, the moment you've all been waiting for (a few whistles and catcalls), *Number 3 on your songsheets: " Why am I always the Bridesmaid?".* Mica holds up [Oh no he ISN'T!] . After two choruses for the audience to learn the tune, on from the wings came Johan and Anton.

The trio

The audience were hysterical. A chorus from the trio. *"And now, Ladies and Gentlemen, chiefly YOURSELVES!"*

§　§　§

The second wedding took place in Gloucestershire and I was the Father of the Bride. I detected some nervousness regarding my speech. I remember the one I had prepared for my son's wedding being confiscated. His sisters were unanimous: "Dad!! You can't say any of that!" Which was a shame because I thought it was some of the funniest stuff I'd ever written. I wasn't too popular for including it in my first memoir 'Westbury Meets East'. It's there if you're sufficiently curious.

Here are some extracts from my much more sober approach.

"In spite of previous experience of my speech-writing, Eleanor bravely insisted that she still wanted me to speak at her wedding but you'll be pleased to know that she imposed three conditions. Firstly, I am to say only nice things about the Bride and Groom, sticking to the topic and listing their best points and talents – no difficulty about that – it shouldn't take long; which fulfils the second condition to keep it short. Thirdly, as a precaution, to run it past Claire, her elder sister, beforehand. Please relax everybody – it has been vetted.

"It is not often in life that a father gets the chance to stand up in public and say out loud how proud he is of one of his children and I should say immediately in parenthesis that I am proud of them all.

"Eleanor was our third child so we were not exactly inexperienced parents. Her brother and sister had provided us with some heart-stopping moments and so we were pretty sure that worrying about her was likely to be part of the deal. In fact, their baby sister gave us very little to worry about, once, that is, at the age of four she stopped crying. From then on, and I hope Eleanor will forgive the cliché, she was as bright as a button, her formal education culminating in a first class honours degree at Canterbury.

"So to Bristol where, her student lifestyle having been a huge influence, she was house-sharing with mates all through her twenties and beyond. I still mistake her for a fresher.

"Always seeking the acquisition of new skills, Eleanor has added an eclectic range to her already talented repertoire so that they now include drystone walling, jewellery-making, proof-reading and copy-editing, paragliding, mosaics design, colour-printing, stone-carving and enamelling. She also swims and plays the flute though not at the same time. She has very, very recently taken on the challenge of what might be called husbandry.

"Of the groom I know very little, apart from his Christian name; we have only met twice before this weekend and shared only brief moments. Immediately I took him to…I'm sorry I'll read that again! Immediately I took to him and we quickly established a modest rapport for it emerged that we share the same good taste in the make of motor car we drive and we have identical views on sport when it comes to streaking. Other qualities that recommend him are his wonderfully dry sense of humour and the fact that he adores Eleanor.

"I am a strong believer in making your own luck and I have no fears for these two because this seems to be exactly what they are doing: making joint decisions and planning together their path through life, combining their considerable talents in a challenging world.

[To Eleanor] "OK so far? Just look at her – absolutely gorgeous!

"I am hardly in a position to proffer matrimonial advice but I could pass on two practical tips that have come my way: the first is from the rule-book of the International School for Butler Administrators: "Make lists – don't trust to memory!". The second …? I forgot to write it down.

"With just a little more than two minutes of the allotted time at my disposal I thought I would treat you to a couple of choruses of my now celebrated and much-loved performance of "Why Am I Always The Bridesmaid?" …but luckily for you I've left the wig and make-up in the car.

"Instead, may I ask you to raise your glasses in a toast to the Bride & Groom. On behalf of everyone present, I wish you lifelong happiness –

"Eleanor & Christian".

§   §   §

Mark and Katy's wedding was in Hampshire. I am Katy's stepfather and I prepared a speech in case I was invited to speak. When I saw the table plan and that I was seated behind a pillar I knew the score. Here it is anyway.

"Bride & Groom, their parents, fellow guests,

"Today, all over this green and pleasant land, epitomised by this beautiful neck of the woods, Bridegrooms, Best Men and Fatners of the Bride – I'm sorry, that's a bad "h" ; I'll read that again. Bridegrooms, Best Men and Fathers of the Bride have all been worrying about their speeches. When I get up to speak other people do the worrying! "What is he going to say?" I was actually forbidden to speak at my own son's wedding. Try and relax.

"Some of us, Katy and Mark included, were together recently at the marriage in Sweden of James and Hannah who, too, are here, maybe on the way to being three by now, we have our fingers crossed. Any or all of the guests at a Swedish wedding have the opportunity to speak if they wish, which makes for a very long banquet because no eating is allowed during the speeches, the soporific effect of which, together with the anaesthetic influence of the alcohol, means that the speeches seem to be getting longer when all they are really getting is slower.

"The trouble with liquid lunches is that they play havoc with one's continence. Shorry. Consonants. I was talking over lunch recently with a Parisienne friend of mine. She has downgraded and moved to my part of France. She'd rather be in Cannes; she says the Dordogne is prone to disasters. She was complaining to me over two matters: her Italian lover was wanting; or rather, she was wanting and not getting. Anyway her other problem was the hot weather which was attracting mosquitoes to her bedroom. I offered to fix her up with a moustiquaire, a mosquito net. I was surprised really when she responded positively to my suggestion. But my pronunciation by that time had fallen victim to several doses of a '98 réserve from the nearby Pauillac vineyards. She thought a musketeer an excellent idea just as long as he was a good shot!

"I hope Mark and Katy will be happy together. I know nothing of Mark except that he's excellent company – that is to say, he doesn't interrupt. Katy, on the other hand… Well with Katy I am better acquainted – we have grown up together. She is a young lady who invites superlatives. She is the most… she is the MOST!

Her step-sister Claire, she's on the table with me over there behind the pillar, kindly reminded me recently that when Katy was very small she exuded a distinctly fetid aroma. The cause was entirely invisible but there was something there, unquestionably, and it had an impressive reach. Politeness was observed within the family in case she should develop a complex. Years passed by until one day her mother decided to involve the medical profession for which she had an inexplicably high regard which remains to this day. After two in-depth sessions with probes and searchlights up Katy's nostrils, the ENT consultant drew a blank. I've thought about that; how do you draw a blank? Finally he sent in a tracker dog [make excited doggy noises] *who located and retrieved (that's what they're trained to do) from a long way back both in distance and time the putrefied remains of an eraser, missing all this while from the end of a favourite pencil. It's a wonder the poor child could think.*

"Naturally we all thought that with the location and removal of the badness Katy would become a better person but at the State school where her sister Gemma had risen to deputy head prefect, Katy became leader of the rebels getting into all sorts of scrapes and excelling only in trouble-making and rolling her own. Academically it looked as if she was not going to make it and her mother decided it was time to transfer her to the pastoral care of Mother Mary Lime-Juice at St Joseph's convent where… she became leader of the rebels getting into all sorts of scrapes. The difference was that she was now in the Town Centre and she and her cronies could set up on the corner of Broad Street chalking up the starting prices for Newbury Races and taking bets.

"Thank you for letting me have my fun. Believe as much or as little of this as you like. Katy, the youngest of the five, did have the toughest struggle. She went on to university and obtained her degree like the others who had been a tough act for her to follow. It's not hard to picture her, as a student in Leeds, striding into the pubs and pushing through the locals to order "a pint o' Tetleys and a bowl o' water fer me whippet" in the local accent.

"She'll go far; I hope they both do. Good luck Mark and Katy!"

...and a Funeral

18th November 2002

THERE CAN BE NO MORE apt word than triste *to describe today's events and so I shall hesitate, in future, before going to use it solely to describe the weather – though that, too, could hardly have been sadder and was, as it were,* sur mesure. *It was the day that Saint Hyroïde la Glande paid its respects and bade farewell to one of its best loved* fermiers, *the day we buried Georges Lafarge. He would have been 79 on December the 1st.*

On Tuesday last he had been seen out driving the smaller tractor with Tommy the sheep-dog on the back as usual. On Thursday he fell into a coma and was taken to the General Hospital at Périgueux .

By nine o'clock in the evening of the following day he had stopped breathing.

§ § §

Monsieur Georges, as I had permission to call him, had had a year's reprieve. The doctors' warning came last autumn just before les vendanges.

The 'setback', to use one of the medical profession's euphemisms, was a prostate cancer and the family was told. They all assumed he didn't know; but he knew. He told me all about it (more than once) during one of our many chats in the lane with much pointing and rummaging in the pocket of his trousers – followed by the shrug at which he excelled.

I can call to mind the morning last October when, with tears in his eyes he stood frustratedly inactive at the edge of the vineyard, obeying doctors' orders as he watched some thirty neighbours busy harvesting his grapes. He believed he was witnessing his last récolte *but, after a few weeks in a convalescent home and a few more walking about with a stick to give him confidence, he was increasingly out and about. He seemed on excellent form throughout the spring and summer, delivering tractor-bucket loads of rocks to my neighbours' courtyard in the hope of a chat, as well as windfalls and other produce to my own door for the same purpose. And he lived to participate in one more grape harvest at the end of September.*

§ § §

Today was a day that might have been choreographed by one of those directors of film noir. A pall of thick mist shrouded the plateau so that "as far as the eye could see" was no further than 30 metres away. The cortège led by a light blue camionette bearing the coffin and crammed with wreaths, was followed by a convoi vraiment exceptionnel, on the normally empty country roads, halting spasmodically to allow other vehicles to nose in from each side of the route; then left at the crossroads and down past his old schoolhouse and directly to the cimetière for the interment – NO service. This was how he wanted it and, preferably, without the congregation!

His only other request was for Tommy to be present; Tommy, who would no longer hear the old man's commands of "Viens!" and "Tiens!" as they worked the troupeaux on the sloping pastures surrounding the farm; the farm which the diminutive one-eyed Serge, the only son, is now left to run, with Marie-Hélène, his wife and Vincent, the grandson, a handsome youth who could be mistaken for his grandfather as a young man in the handful of sepia photographs taken during and immediately after the Second World War and kept proudly in a small drawer with his other keepsakes. How long these three remain under the same roof will be a meaty topic for speculation among the gossip-mongers (of whom there is no shortage) because it is widely known that Serge is being energetically cuckolded by the burly but extremely fit Henri Legrand whose attentions probably explain the well-built Marie-Hélène's permanent grin. Since her father-in-law's first illness, it is clear that she has been embracing with enthusiasm her new role of La Bergère in all its aspects, above and beyond the sheep!

As if on cue, the fine rain arrived at the same time as the mourners and a few motley umbrellas were poked into the sky to direct the drizzle into the ears and down the necks of the unprotected. The coffin was manoeuvred into the Lafarge family sarcophagus – a monument in grey marble of quite unexpectedly grand proportions given the modest size of their living quarters – by six attendants in ill-fitting jackets of a slightly grubbier blue to that of the van that had brought them. There was an uncertain pause; but no eulogy or tribute of any sort was forthcoming which, even at an affaire civile, is highly unusual. But then, with a little local knowledge one realises firstly, that the Lafarge and Bonnet families have been at loggerheads for generations; secondly, that Monsieur Hervé Bonnet is currently Maire de Saint Hyroïde la Glande and thirdly, it is customarily the maire who addresses those gathered...

With the rain still persisting, any possible dismay at the lack of protocol soon dissolved and we all filed past the open doors of the tomb, muttered our condoléances to the tearful Serge and Vincent (no sign of Marie-Hélène – nor of Henri Legrand come to think of it) and ran quickly to our cars for shelter. A turnout in excess of one hundred. But Georges, looking down, would not have failed to notice a particular absence – that of his best friend – and to have given one of his shrugs...
The Good Shepherd – May he Rest in Peace.

Chapter Three
Making Things Clear

February 2003

I AM FLAT ON MY BACK on a hospital trolley. A variety of ventilator grilles and lighting diffusers stare back like blank over-sized tick-boxes awaiting my choice from a selection of ceiling tiles – I like that pattern best, in the Japanese *ryokan* style – as I am propelled along corridor after corridor of fire-appliances and nursing-stations on the journey to the operating theatre. Fabrice, the porter, is in a tearing rush to beat his rivals to the lift, deftly handling the *chicanes* – he should enter us in the *luge* – but now that the Big Day is upon me and a certain amount of apprehension has built up, I would appreciate it more if he'd go at it in less of a hurry. On the other hand, dressed in this ludicrous hide-nothing gown (another hark-back to the *ryokan*) and wearing a huge matching hide-abso-lutely-everything blue elasticated paper hat and, therefore looking and feeling a total pillock, I do see the virtue of getting this whole thing over and done with.

§ § §

Two months ago I went for a routine eye-test. Everyone who knows me and a few who don't have put up with me raving about the beautiful view that goes with the derelict farmhouse I'm renovating in the *Périgord Noir*. Recently I noticed that it had got a bit blurred and I thought I probably needed new specs. It turned out that a cataract was caking up my right eye. "You are not ill" insisted the *ophthalmologue*, "but you are deteriorating." [Nice chap] "I can cheat Nature by writing you a prescription for some new lenses and then, later, when you feel ready, I can blitz the cataract and restore your vision, though you will still require glasses, either for reading or for long range. The timing is entirely up to you."

Two weeks later, though, I was back in the consulting-room asking for the offending evidence of deterioration to be removed. It transpired that, rather curiously, whilst a change of lenses to my spectacles would not be covered by my *mutuelle* (private health top-up insurance), everything concerned with the cataract operation would. So I wouldn't be out of pocket and the surgeon would be significantly nearer to affording his next thoroughbred racehorse. Contrary to the old adage, it certainly *does* pay to cut corneas. I came away with a date inked in and a sheet of information regarding his Clinic in Périgueux (what you might call a site for sore eyes).

It dawned on me that I would not be able to drive myself away after the op. So, when my girlfriend offered to take me in her car, stay with me overnight if I so wished and then drive me home, I decided to splash out and book double accommodation. With all the premiums I had paid it might even the score. The preliminary paper-work also revealed the need for an appointment with the anaesthetist which required a prior appointment with a cardiologist and another at the Centre de Biologie Médicale for a blood test and the issue of a *carte de groupe sanguin* carried by all people with any sense but not many English! Do YOU know YOUR blood type? And in order to be *remboursé* for these apparently essential documents I also needed, to support my claim, procedural prescriptions from my local G.P. to make it all kosher – more charges, of course, but then pedigree retrievers come expensive too and yes, my doctor hunts.

While I was wired up in the Francheville Dept. of Cardiology, the specialist chatted away at length on the subject of vintage wines on which he was very well informed. They all have expensive hobbies, these medics, and so once again it was no surprise to be faced with a colossal bill for on-the-spot payment. Not wishing to let such an expensive piece of paper out of my sight, I personally escorted the cardiogram to the anaesthetist's luxury suite to be interviewed and to have my blood pressure taken. This was the first time I'd been subjected to a medical "interview" which amounts to being asked to complete a form running to several pages of questions to which you've to answer "Oui" or "Non". I've been extremely lucky healthwise so it took next to no time at all. They couldn't believe the list of no's; in fact I'd go as far as to say they were disappointed and they really tut-tutted when I couldn't name my blood group. To atone, I hastened over to the Laboratoire behind the Palais de Justice. The zone was swarming with police. Citizens less law-abiding than me had obviously made themselves scarce – how else to account for the unusually plentiful number of parking spaces? I found the building easily. Inside, the attractive *biologiste* for the blood test replied cheerfully but unoptimistically to my question regarding reimbursement and her "*Je suis très désolée*", as she jabbed her needle into me while wearing a dazzling but contradictory smile, was far from convincing. But then she explained that she found a smile was the best way to cope in a job that involved making holes in people all day long! Anyway I came away with another important piece of paper.

There is a *bouchon* (traffic jam) in the pre-operative bay where I've been parked and then abandoned by Fabrice. Looking round I would think I am the youngest here by a substantial margin [I'm 60-something] although the consultant claimed he'd had cataract patients as young as forty. It is said that they are doing these operations every five minutes. Anyway there is quite a queue and I should estimate that by lunchtime Monsieur le docteur Court-Maison [trans. Short-House; a military expression] will have enough left over for a yacht. He is definitely looking very chipper. He has been over to say "Bonjour" and to squirt some more dilator in my eye. His sadistic lineswoman has had numerous goes at jamming a catheter into me, finally succeeding on what felt like the nineteenth attempt. Her age suggests that she's not still learning the job so I suppose she's simply anti-men. After an interminable wait there's another change of ceiling-scape and a really gorgeous sexy blonde comes and shoves a needle into me. Men-haters every one. [Actually, I was told later that this one was on her third divorce. Perhaps they're bad pickers…but there's really no need to take it out on the rest of us.]

More ceiling tiles and I'm surrounded by three masked figures clad in green. Giggles from two of them (I imagine my gown has slipped) while the third sets up the phaco-emulsification apparatus and a sort of miniature tent over the left side of my head. Now a familiar voice: "Please tell me if you can feel this." Ouch. Yes. It just comes home to me that this is going to be done under a local anaesthetic. "I'm putting a reverse clamp over your right eye to keep it open…" seems reasonable "…during the removal of the *cristallin*…" doesn't that mean 'lens'?! "…by cutting it into four pieces and taking out the fragments one at a time." Gulp. "Let us know if at any stage you need to cough. This is very important." What about sneezing? "Then, when the capsule is rinsed clean I shall secure your implant." First time that's been mentioned. I thought you were just going to scrape off the cataract. Too late to change my mind?

During the forty or so minutes that followed (the sensation is best described as having a small bird pecking away inside your eyeball), a robotic voice from inside the emulsifier confirms completion of each step of the procedure. Not comfortable at all. I was then trundled out to the recovery room and jammed in among a dozen or so inert forms on parallel rows of trolleys. I willed them to move or speak or show any reassuring sign that I hadn't wound up in the forensic department. Then, by turning my head, my left eye spied a pretty nurse sitting in front of a monitor and she sent me a smile. And I dozed…

§ § §

As they were still struggling with the matter of bed availability (they are snowed under and this is the private sector, don't forget; they must be coining it !), I was wheeled down at lunchtime to the Reception Floor where, re-united with my belongings and curtained off from public gaze in a pleasant cubicle with a view overlooking a park, I consumed a 3-course meal, a bit industrial but very welcome after my fast. It included a glass of Bergerac Rouge served by a rather jolly middle-aged lady who introduced herself as "Marie". "I shall call you '*Mon Ange*'", I said; whereupon she insisted that she was more of a Virgin (Marie, you see) than an Angel. I'm afraid the look of wonder must have shown on my face and then, in my embarrassment, I made things worse by saying quickly and, I hoped, admiringly that one didn't come across many of those these days. She laughed at my confusion and said what she meant was that her birthday was on the 18th September which made her a *Vierge* (Virgo in English. Whoops.). So…? Better leave it there.

It's tea-time and I'm still marooned in Transit. A young lady in a white coat comes to check I haven't gone missing. She shows surprise when I ask if it would be OK for me to change out of the cheeky little number and into my own clothes. She thinks about it for a moment, weighing up the litigious implications, then says "*Oui, vous avez le droit*"("You have the right!").

At about five o'clock I am finally escorted to a double room. I un-pack my stuff and lay out Fanny's night things, slippers, etc. to make her feel welcome later. At six o'clock the door opens and I turn to greet her. Instead, in come Monsieur et Madame Dysfunctional and their daughter Delphine looking as though they have broken out from a refugee camp. Fanny's pyjamas are tossed to one side by hospital staff who are talking deferentially to these intruders. It soon becomes clear that they are no strangers to their surroundings and that the old man on crutches has already had three months' worth of hip and knee replacement surgery in this very clinic. They are making a fuss because they are accustomed to having a room to themselves and his wife has been told that there will be no place for her tonight. "*Les malades réguliers devraient avoir la priorité*", says he. The situation is not improved by the arrival of a folding camp-bed for Fanny. I am beginning to realise that one night in this place is going to be one night too many. *L'atmosphère est très tendue* (strained).

For supper, lunch is served again, even down to the identical wine. In what might be taken for a peace offering, Guy encourages me to take his unwanted *tomates farcies* of which I've already consumed a surfeit today so "*Merci, non.*"

His family having departed, the ambiance improves and by the time Fanny arrives, he and I have begun to talk to each other. He is 79 years old and at 17 stone far too heavy for his load-bearing joints. He was born in Badefols d'Ans – the village approximately four kilometres from where I live and which sits picturesquely in my view from the terrace. He left at the age of 4 and has never considered going back because, he says, it's in *les picadis*; but that's exactly what I like about it.

The door opens and, immaculately dressed in expensive English tweeds, his orthopaedic surgeon enters and with eyes like Euro signs he greets Guy as though he is an old friend. He holds X-rays to the light to reveal an impressive amount of *quincaillerie* (ironmongery; one of the first words I learned when I came on an exchange to Brittany at the age of 15). I take this opportunity to assure Fanny that I will understand perfectly well if she baulks at the prospect of this regrettable *ménage à trois* and would prefer to return in the morning but she seems not to want to miss out on what might be a good yarn to share with her colleagues at work. We shall be strange bedfellows, that's for sure.

§ § §

8th February 2003

With an eye shield over one eye, Fanny has started referring to me as her *"Corsaire"*. The *cauchemar* began soon after lights-out; a truly metaphorical use of the word because I didn't actually get to sleep at all. Not a wink, not even for the available eye. In spite of his boast of knowing his way around, Guy was either bumping into the furniture in the dark on his frequent trips to the lavatory or else flooding the room with (no wait a moment, please) flooding the room with light by pulling on the switchcord instead of the one to heave himself up from the bed. There was a distinctive rattle and creak from his *cannes anglaises* (French for crutches!) and he needed them for even the shortest distance. But in addition to that, both my room-mates had very impressive snores, although Guy won on decibels the way a warthog, say, would outshine a dormouse. The dormouse's dainty rhythms had more variety; the warthog's rasping crescendos lacked any redeeming subtlety whatsoever. They both took it in turns to keep me awake. But he fired farts as well.

By the time the day-nurse arrived with her insincere inquiry *comme un perroquet*, I'd had plenty of time to rehearse a reply: *"Écoutez, c'était un vrai cauchemar ici; c'était comme un choeur de sangliers qui grognaient toute la nuit!"* ("It's been a nightmare here – like a chorus of snuffling wild boar all night long.")

Breakfast was the usual non-meal.

At 10 a.m. I was ushered downstairs to the doctor's office where he removed the bandages [AMAZING MOMENT], examined his handiwork, shook my hand and presented me with the *coque* (eyeshield) as though it was a trophy. Next patient. On my way out I politely asked if he was off-duty for the rest of the weekend and he said as soon as he had finished he was flying to Kerry to look at some bloodstock.

He'll see me next month to prescribe lenses for new reading glasses. In the meantime, the leafless winter trees are showing sharp and clear on the distant horizon and my sight is young again.

§ § §

A year and a half later

The argument is that previous experience works to your advantage but I can affirm that this is not always the case. Certainly you may feel prepared and relaxed from knowing fully what to expect the "second time around" and therefore face the operation with confidence; but equally you might approach the repetition with trepidation knowing what you do. Such thoughts were in my head as the day loomed when the ophthalmologist was to use his skills on this other cataract and I was, frankly, apprehensive. The first operation, whilst successful, had been very uncomfortable and I was thinking more along the lines of "forewarned is forewarned". [Taken from Westbury's Book of Proverbs Revisited. Other examples: "a change is as good as a change"and "two can live as cheaply as two."]

Anyway, I'm lying here unhappily on the hospital trolley in the ante-room of the Clinique du Parc operating theatre, waiting for the anaesthetist, when masked figures gather round. One of them pokes his finger in my eye. Charming! Then propels me into the sterile space, no injection, no anything. Hang on, I think to myself. If I'm having to go through the same bird-pecking-out-my-eye sensation like last time I'd very much appreciate some sort of pain relief! Feebly I enquire: "Um, is this correct? Shouldn't I be anaesthetised?"

"*Ne vous inquiètez pas*", replies the *chirugien.* "*Nous avons mis du gel sur votre oeil.*" Well, I tell myself, they've got to do better than that. Isn't gel what the young men use these days to make their hair stick up all spikey. What use is that going to be?! But the procedure has begun.

Nothing is the same. In the eighteen months since they dealt with the right eye, the format has been changed. Apart, that is, from the immediately recognisable recorded metallic female voiceover that announces the commencement and completion of each stage. Instead of going in through the centre front, the surgeon will make a sneaky sideways approach (there has never been any use of the verb "to cut") through the left wall of the eye. This, I cannot help supposing, will involve rather more than the rolling back and clamping of the eyelid. So no "pecking bird" this time but, as far as I can make out, a probing "push and pull" by two brightly-lit but fuzzy lozenge shapes tweezering away. They seem rather blunt.

Fifteen minutes of this... maybe twenty... maybe ten, then I'm rolled out to the recovery ward to join a dozen or more other recumbent incumbents. Rather inappropriately, Latin dance music is coming from a portable radio close by and the blonde nurse in charge is swaying her hips to the rhythm, perfectly aware that she is being watched. She smiles and sashays over with her clipboard. This she naughtily places flat on my crotch area and starts writing on it! Recovery is quickly achieved.

The porter, Gilles this time, trolleys me through the labyrinth of corridors to the jolting giant cubic yoyo that is the *ascenseur*. More shunting around and I'm finally left in the welcome privacy of my own room, clad as I am in a provocative backless almost transparent number that would grace an Anne Summers catalogue. Perhaps not. Thank goodness the unflattering elasticated hat got lost somewhere on the journey. [I took the opportunity to enquire after Fabrice, the speed merchant I befriended last time. He has been promoted to a geriatric ward where his skills no doubt bring some late excitement into the lives of the patients – "If you're at death's door, he'll pull you through."]

Next morning the night nurse goes happily off duty having liberated my *coque*. Then, downstairs, the doctor checks his handiwork while an imaginary orchestra plays "Don't you roll that bloodshot eye at me" and I am free to go.

Chapter Four
La France Profonde II

Introducing Gilbert

TIMBER BEING ONE OF FRANCE'S principal resources and the Périgord being well off for forests, I had very little difficulty finding sawmills in the vicinity. The main problem has been their slowness to deliver even the most basic of items *sur mesure*. One of the *scieries* that did oblige me quickly with some of my more straightforward stuff like lintels (though not always straight, it has to be said), was owned by a certain Gilbert Banneyx (pronounced Zjeelbair Banaykes) who I got to know quite well. He was a one-man band. Although in his eighties, he could not face up to the idea of retirement and each time I drive through the small town of Fosse-magne on the RN89 I notice that his huge *atelier* doors are pushed wide open for business.

In the course of time our transactions became more and more like sociable occasions as the invitations to join him at the "*heure de l'apéro*" became part of the routine. I met his missus, a Norah Batty look-alike, never out of her curlers and who always stood listening while the two of us sat at the kitchen table exchanging travellers' tales. He had toured China on his own, a fact of which he was rather proud. Some of his stories took some believing (but then so did some of mine); others were rather saucy but his wife just joined in the laughter. He it was who taught me the phrase "*jolie nana*" when I told him I had a French girlfriend; and he called me a "*chaud lapin*" – hot rabbit! I took it as a compliment.

Once, I found myself leaving after dark. We had started on the home-made *pineau* at about 4p.m. He insisted on drawing me a map on a scrap of paper so that I could avoid the main road and any keen gendarmes that might be on late duty. Tractor tracks and gaps in hedges were confidently pencilled in but where he went wrong (and where, you have already guessed, I eventually went wrong) was in his estimates of distance so that I would keep to the edge of a field, eyes peeled for the exit point, but find myself back at where I came in and have to start again. After the third field I was in hysterics.

Every now and then there was a clunk as the low-slung Audi stumbled over a rock and I thought what a miserable owner I was to be mistreating her this way. At some stage my calculations took me into a farmyard. Dogs barked at me. Hunched over the wheel, the Richard III soliloquy came into my head.

I abandoned his map when I came to a lane for which he hadn't allowed. So: left or right? How can you rely on your sense of direction when you've lost all sense of everything else: time, proportion and humour among them. I should have gone left. Nothing prepared me for the ford… but I braked in time. Phew. Quite sobering. The moon came out and helped me reverse into an opening that looked familiar but I stuck to the lane. After a bit I reached a crossroads with a signpost and all became clear. I was still in France.

I collapsed into bed at 1 a.m. Some time during the night I realised I'd left my lintels at the sawmill.

§ § §

ALL THE FUN OF THE *FOIRE*

15th October 2003

My little partly-restored *fermette* is right in the flight-path of the *grues*. The cranes flew south during the night making a terrific commotion as though He'd sent His chariot but the birds were squabbling over the address. Summer is over and winter looms. It was announced on the moaning news that there had been an increase in the influenza epidemic: so you could say that the *grues* flew and the 'flu grew! [But you don't have to.]

The octogenarian Gilbert and his septuagenarian "back-with-his-first-wife" buddy Alain plus my comparatively youthful self made an unlikely trio recently on the occasion of the *Foire de Saint Firmin* at Le Buisson-Cadouin, the other side of Le Bugue. I had a strong feeling that it was normally Alain who drove and that I had been roped in just so that each of them could drink copiously to their livers' delight and Alain's *permis de conduire* would not be put at risk.

This fair is one of the very few remaining in France that can boast the inclusion of a horse/cattle/sheep market amongst all the usual A to Z of stalls selling everything from vegetables to haberdashery, so that would be asparagus to zips. They expected me to show interest in the animals, after all I looked the part in my country squire attire, but I've already made reference to an incident at a riding-school in Whetstone, where a fiend of a horse called Jet, who was built like a destrier, trod on my foot whilst still in the stable, since when I've not felt the least inclination to get nearer to these beasts than a furlong or two.

Having experienced a number of these *foires*, I can recognise a recurring pattern. There is always a leather goods stall with no customers and a seated scowling salesperson muttering to himself. Regardless of the size of these markets, there is always a minimum of three stalls selling socks. Only socks. Is there any other nation that abandons its socks in such an off-foot manner ? They can't possibly wear them out because nobody walks anywhere: they're either in their cars driving like maniacs or on their *vélos* wobbling three abreast in front of you. You never see a farmer on foot; he takes his tractor everywhere. It's true: it's safer *not* to walk! So how do you explain the need for such a huge supply of socks…unless they're left behind in hasty departures.

This particular fair had a joker shouting out *"Chaussettes pour les travailleurs"* ("Socks for the Workers!"). When we came into sight he carried on *"et pour eux qui ne travaillent pas!"* ("…and for those who don't work!") I bought six eggs I didn't need from two little old ladies who earnestly assured me they were fresh, the eggs, that is, not the little old ladies, the one being a grandmother and the other a great granny at least. They were nevertheless full of smiles and *bonhomie* and giggled at my flirting. I should be locked up.

A demonstrator of high-powered miniature expensive vacuum-cleaners was completely demoralised in mid-patter by Gilbert's loud and witty asides that the crowd found more entertaining. There was a percussive contribution from a drummer who had been strolling between the stalls and getting in everyone's way, lending a bizarre contrast to the otherwise rural ambiance of the occasion and certainly drawing more attention to himself than to the traders he was there to advertise. More of him later.

Lunchtime sees us inside the largest *Salle des Fêtes* I've ever come across – imagine an empty factory; that inviting. Row upon row of trestle tables disappeared into the distance, wooden benches ran parallel to the long sides. It could have been a transit station for refugees. No amount of *apéritif* consumption was going to deaden the awfulness of the *repas* though we did make the effort. In a further attempt to anaesthetise the situation, I splashed out on some of the labelled wine on sale but it was only very slightly more bearable than the anonymous stuff that was included in the ticket The meal was best forgotten as quickly as possible. It was brought ready-plated from somewhere out of sight (and might once have been warm) by a team of jolly ladies who had obviously been recruited to divert attention away from the food. My inebriated randy companions, who had insisted that we sat together, were soon chatting up the young *serveuses* with lines like "Are you looking for us?" and "Do you live at home with your parents?" Embarrassing. To be outshone, that is.

The drummer had re-appeared and his drum-rolls seemed to coincide with every one of Gilbert's *bons mots* but, come the tombola, he had climbed upon the stage and they became more frequent and prolonged as numbers were called and winners took time checking their tickets before braving the obstacle course to collect what they'd won. A handshake from the drummer seemed every bit a part of the prize. Dressed in a military khaki tunic with medals and a Général de Gaulle style peaked hat, he would have been more impressive if he had not been so short. It was hard to tell if his black curly moustache was real or false but he was such a card he had me splitting my sides. At the end of each riff he leaned forward from the waist in a half bow, turning this way and that and beaming to one and all, his drumsticks now hanging from loosely swinging arms. Then it was time for the speeches and there was still no stopping him! The mayor's every pause was punctuated by short rapid tattoos – as if to mask the fact that nobody was applauding. It was clearly the drummer's show and he was having a ball. As far as I'm concerned, he saved the day.

Chapter Five
Mostly "All that jazz" – some notes!

ON THE CORNER OF *RUE Gambetta* and the *Boulevard Montaigne* in the county town of Périgueux was a beautiful *fin-de-siècle* building with a gorgeously elaborate *fer forgé* balcony running round the front and side. Inside, at first floor level, was a jazz venue called the *Jaune Poussin.* I had the good fortune to be introduced to it very soon after arriving to start my life in France.

It was a welcome distraction from caravan living and I spent quite a lot of time there listening to some great jazz and eating some food *pas du tout mal* in this splendid establishment run in cabaret-dinner-dance fashion by the stylish Gérard Caillé and his family. Françoise, his wife, known as Fan-Fan, sang and their daughter Alex was in charge of the catering and just about everything else. A cook, barman and a few *serveuses* were engaged for the major attractions which were usually trios or quartets (no room for anything larger) seemingly made up of musicians who had, for the most part, met together for the first time that day. But the results were great. The atmosphere was informal, intimate even and the whole thing was proof positive that it is not necessary for jazz to be housed in a basement.

Jazz Upstairs

I think the most memorable of the *dîner-concerts* was one featuring a black American singer called Nancy Holloway, seriously older in appearance than the publicity photo but a great performer nonetheless. She was billed as "The singer-songwriter" and turned out to have composed the music and lyrics of "Fever". She was nearing the end of her tour and was losing her voice; as a consequence it became, literally, a low key affair. Notwithstanding, she managed to

---

croak a number of standards before murdering "Fever", which was a great shame. Then she attempted to strangle the pianist because, she complained, she couldn't work with an accompanist who didn't drink. [Pierre Calligaris had accompanied Fan-Fan for years, hit a bad patch and was now drying out.] To complete the backing trio there was the resident *contrebasse*, Daniel Amelot and the *batteur*, Ivan Capelle (on the right in the picture) nicknamed "Captain Grisou" – *grisou* is French for methane i.e. explosive. Looking as though he'd slept under a bridge was a surprisingly twinkly guest clarinettist, Philippe le Presseiac, he's not in the photo, who took some of the pressure off the main attraction by amusing us with his Louis Armstrong and Jean-Gabin-as-Quasimodo impersonations out of a face borrowed from W.C.Fields. Great entertainment..

Then amazingly, "La Holloway" walked over to me and asked me to dance! Of course, it was a way to give her voice a rest from singing. As far as I was concerned she could take as long as she liked – I hadn't had a woman in my arms for over a fortnight. We chatted about this and that. I was going to ask her how she felt about sharing a name with a women's prison and then I didn't. A photo-journalist fussed around.

§ § §

The minute I arrived at the *Jaune Poussin* a couple of weeks later, Gérard presented me with a photo of myself and Ms Holloway! This, it turned out, fitted perfectly across the three central columns of the front page of that day's New York Herald Tribune. I added a typewritten caption:

'Nancy Holloway dances with the duc d' Anlhiac. Jaune Poussin, Friday.'

and posted photocopies to family and friends. Nobody twigged!

On another occasion the upright piano had been magicked away in order to make space for a quintet consisting of soprano sax, trombone, tuba, guitar and drums; all new faces to me. They played a lot of Sydney Bechet numbers that got better and better as *they* got used to each other and we got used to *them*. But the guy who, for me, up-staged *every*body was the American, Gary Kiser, who had traded in the advertised tuba for a 12-kilo souzaphone which he played with great finesse and imagination and a kind of bobbing motion. He did everything except make love to it, although come to think of it maybe that's exactly what he *was* doing! The ambiance worked its magic on my guests, too, and they were captivated. We motored back to my hilltop and sat sipping nightcaps until 3a.m.

Now it's true that the food at the *Jaune Poussin* wasn't out of this world and that applied to the toilet facilities, too (there was just the one) but all was forgiven because of the great jazz and the intimacy of the environment. Then the building became due for demolition, victim to so-called planners. On that site there now stands a modern block housing yet another bank; the wonderful cabaret atmosphere has been lost in the rubble. The Caillé family re-located to what had been a bowling alley in the rue Président Wilson. It has been completely gutted, re-decorated and equipped with a modern kitchen and 4-star toilets but there is no disguising its rectangular shape and its lack of intimacy, although the usual warm welcome hasn't changed and there have been a few evenings when we were delighted to see familiar faces among the musicians, too, particularly a band calling themselves Les Haricots Rouges who had an excellent repertoire mixing swing and humour and a banjoist who tip-toed precariously the entire length of the laden dinner-tables while playing. But, true to the last line of their chorus finale, it was soon "La Fin des Haricots!" It's no longer a jazz venue. The very popular *thé dansants* pay the rent today.

Gérard was involved with the Festival Nouvelle Orléans held each August in Périgueux's Parc Gamenson but he was eventually ousted, victim to politics and jealousy. Whereupon the programming suffered or, to be more exact, evenings of Gospel-singing are not my thing at all. Following what turned out to be the last performance I attended, I made some notes. "The opener was an American solo pianist called David Paquette who had arrived from New Zealand where it is possible he wowed the sheep. An ageing pony-tailed hippie he showed no sign of letting the next act on to the stage; he just kept on hogging it and he gave the sound technicians a terrible time. But it was actually the poor sound quality throughout the evening that gave a certain *unity* to the whole show. Next, our ears were assaulted by the over-amplified sounds of somebody called Eugene "Hideaway" Bridges, a black (and blues) guitarist who unfortunately did not live up to his nickname. He, too, was pointedly disgusted with the sound system yet he repeatedly showed interest as to whether we in the audience were enjoying ourselves which was very thoughtful of him but a shade lacking in sensitivity. The *dénouement* was by someone with the Irakli name of unlikely. He led the Tuxedo Big Band in a Tribute to Louis Armstrong. Well, in truth he wasn't always in the lead as it developed into a bit of a race as to who could get home first. The guest trumpeter, looking like an older, slimmer and taller version of Mel Brooks, had been on tour celebrating the 100th birthday year of the Father of Jazz. His tiredness wasn't too obvious and his French was good. Well, he *was* French, actually. The conductor, who doubled on saxophone, was a young man who bore a strong resemblance to Oscar Wilde as played by Stephen Fry. To distinguish him from the other players, all wearing *le smoking* (black tuxedos), *his* jacket was in a subtle shade of white. The drummer sang better than the singer but then we didn't get to hear how the singer drummed. The singer's awkwardness on stage was explained by the dress she nearly wore. The whole ensemble could have done with a choreographer and more time in rehearsal. They tried to emulate the Big Band practice where sections of the orchestra stand up and sit down in unison. It is the same word in French (*à l'unisson*) so there was really no excuse for the shambles. The signals would have been marked on the sheet music but then, if they were all travelling at different speeds...*there's* the explanation. To be perfectly fair they were not helped by the amateurs in charge of the sound equipment. Eventually someone backstage took mercy on us all and covered them in artificial smoke. Undeterred or discouraged, the band stoically went ahead with an unrequested encore, "When the Saints Go Marching In" (one they could play in the dark).

§ § §

For *three* consecutive summers I went along to some of the jazz concerts offered by the Festival du Pays d'Ans. The first was scheduled to be held in the gardens of Tourtoirac Abbey but inclement weather sent it indoors to the Salle des Fêtes. A huge ugly barn of a building, lined inside consistently with huge ugly tiling, it was packed. Good sign, I thought. After a few bars, though, I was planning to slip away at an opportune moment but I had chosen to sit towards the middle of a long row so was obliged to wait for the interval. There was no interval. It was purgatory. The percussionist was on an ego-trip and the music was ten times worse than Stan Kenton.

The following year with fine weather and a different line-up, it was held outside in the Abbey gardens, a beautiful location but the jazz was once again excruciating. Maybe the musicians were the same as before and they'd simply changed the name of the band. Dogs of the neighbourhood gathered to bark their protest at the discord. It was actually very funny. Well at the end of the unbelievably long first number I was able to leave along with a large part of the audience. [It is recorded that the open-air début of Shostakovich's First Symphony was played to the sound of barking dogs. Laughter too, perhaps, but I apologise to any devotees for having made any comparison.]

So why did I go back a third time?! I was pleased to see that *this* was definitely a different bunch. *This* band looked like a bunch of hoods. Their ensemble playing was a cacophony but the piano solos were fantastic. The pianist was probably stoned but the music was great so I sat it out and I don't think anybody actually threw anything.

§ § §

Saint-Robert, just over the border into Corrèze, also holds its own programme of concerts each summer, something for everybody. I've come to the conclusion that, were it not for the influx of tourists, we locals would be left completely devoid of entertainment. [The Théatre Odyssée in Périgueux *is* open all the year round but it caters for an audience of snobs, lovers of dance or for the very young; nothing that says "popular".] So I do try to support these so-called "festivals" as much as I can. Sometimes this can backfire, as it did one year when I paid in advance for three concerts in the Saint-Robert village church and a spell of hay fever prevented me from going to the first. However, in addition to the serious stuff, free musical offerings were advertised on certain afternoons in the church quadrangle and I set about taking advantage of those by way of compensation. They sounded to be more my cup of tea.

Punctual to a fault, I arrived for the first right on time, found a seat in the front but had got the date wrong and finished up having to endure a duo of accordionists. As soon as they'd finished their first number, I waved to an imaginary friend at the back of the audience and retreated. But I persevered and returned the following week to enjoy jazz standards played by a small sextet (just the five of them) led by a slide trombonist whose instrument had a crack in it which produced some unexpected raspberry-like random syncopation. The tuba, the banjoist, the trumpeter and the soprano-saxophone all fought back. It was wonderful, mostly because they were enjoying themselves so much. [I later delivered their business card to Chantal at L'Estaminet, Badefols d'Ans; they would certainly be good enough to alternate with Dr.Bob's band, her regular group.] One week later, the Paul Faure Trio of piano, bass and drums performed as though they were used to playing with a fourth. Apart from a very heavily disguised interpretation of "All the Things You Are", all the numbers were of the pianist's own composition. I think he was trying to "do a Dave Brubeck" but without a Paul Desmond.

The organiser of all this had introduced all the performances with a very brief speech. Very unusual, this; the brevity, that is. He spoke with the whole of his rather burly body, swaying and gyrating with sudden movements. With his feet close together it gave the impression that he was that one remaining skittle in a bowling alley and very likely to topple over at any moment.

I'd booked two tickets for the next of these treats and Fanny and I decided that, since it was the height of the *canicule* (heat wave) it would be a good idea to first spend the afternoon cooling off in the pool of the Hotel Saint-Robert, where there would be time to enjoy supper before walking over to the church for an evening of poetry and letter-readings by an actress *"très connue"* (well, known to Fanny, anyway) to be accompanied by a pianist and viola. Byron and Berlioz provided the main source material. This, I will admit, was a pretty challenging choice from my point of view but at least it should get us out of this heat. The afternoon passed off well. We dipped our bodies in the pool and sipped chilled *rosé*. At around five o'clock the actress arrived for a swim and then sat at the table next to ours to dry off and to go through the programme with a young lady who turned out to be the pianist. All of which thrilled Fanny who received a nod as an acknowledgement for her adulation. After our supper on the terrace we strolled over to enjoy the recital. The church was like an oven after all and we escaped after the interval.

The last of my advance bookings at Saint-Robert was also an abnormal choice for me. Perhaps I was hoping that someone in the mould of Jacques Loussier could have jazzed up the Bach Cantatas. My reserved seat turned out to be at the back of the sanctuary, the altar steps leading up to the "stage". The musicians filed on first, the men wearing their shirts outside their trousers – the first sign of a declining civilisation I always think. [Remember the Greeks? And the Romans? Nothing tucked in: unsurprising descent into debauchery.] They were followed by the 4-piece choir. Both the tenor and the bass had been to the "sing-with-your-buttocks" academy of music which, from my seat I was well-placed to appreciate. The pretty contralto was more my type although her dress rather resembled borrowed curtains that had to be returned to a very tall window because just below the knee they'd needed to be gathered up like Austrian blinds – very distracting. The handsome soprano kept her *martinet* discreetly out of sight in her music bag. But it was there. Oh yes. Our paths cross from time to time – only in my dreams. I have no recollection of the music whatsoever.

§   §   §

Because of the paucity of live jazz locally I have become more willing to travel further and further afield. In July 2012 I drove to a jazz venue in Ségur le Chateau. The very word jazz would have offended the majority of my forebears but what would have shocked them all the more was the fact of it being played in a church. There turned out to be two parts to the programme because, as a preliminary to the main turn, a small quintet from Bergerac (there were just the four of them – I can never resist my time-worn joke) played Nouvelle Orléans style jazz, mainly standards (Sweet Lorraine, Petite Fleur, etc.) out in the open behind the church but under an awful makeshift black plastic awning as inclement weather had been anticipated. Meantime the audience partook of a buffet supper (for which one paid on an *ad hoc* basis with *ségurins* – pretend money – reminding me of the token money at Bridewell Heath) politely laying down their plastic cutlery to applaud the soloists individually as is customary. As Humphrey Lyttelton once said of Ludovic Kennedy's drumming, "It wasn't ba-ad." They ran late; they always do. An interval of 20 minutes was declared which enabled me to descend to where I'd parked the car, collect the essential cushions, order an espresso in a bar that was about to close but thereby enabling me to gain access to a loo, drink the thimble-full of coffee and climb back up the hill to find my *siège numéroté* in the church.

The cushions always prove to be a good idea. I recognised the same envious looks as those we used to see on the faces of less well organised members of the audience at various school functions in Goring, Pangbourne, Woodley, Theale and Henley all those years ago. Uncomfortable seats were and are still a known drawback at such events. Instead of kneeling on my allocated *prie-dieu*, I sat on it in the Lady Chapel with my back to the statue of the Virgin Mary. It did seem weird.

The twenty minute break grew in length to forty minutes but the trio, on tour from Marseille, finally launched into a tribute to Oscar Petersen. They were excellent but live music in an environment where all around you are reminders of death? The familiar repertoire began to lift my spirits but the better strategy was to close my eyes. *Le Chemin de Croix* tableaux hanging from the walls contributed little to the rendition of "Sometimes I'm Happy", for example. It's true, too, that when you come to think about it, there are certain singers, like Amy Winehouse, Robbie Williams, Grace Jones, etc. all of whom are better with your eyes wide shut. "Being There" summed up the whole point of my journey. I was beginning to really enjoy myself so it was disappointing to say the least when at 10.30pm they announced another interval. Not wanting to risk driving back "In the Wee Small Hours of the Morning" and remembering to gather up my cushions, I left.

§ § §

Thinking back six or seven years, there was an *auberge* in Cherveix-Cubas called Les Charmettes that was run in English pub-style by a crazy Dutch guy and his English wife whose speciality was swearing at each other. In fact the *only* charming aspect about the place, indeed the main attraction, was their under-age daughter, a precocious nymph who waited at table when they held their periodic *soirées*. She certainly distracted from the antics of her parents. But their resident band, Dr Bob and his swing quartet, was a major draw, too, most especially when a tall willowy smokey-voiced vision of a girl joined them to sing covers from the fifties. It was a great loss when the place was sold.

So when I spotted the poster outside La Presse a few days ago…

> "Dr Bob Quartet"
> 30 juillet 18.00 – 21.00
> Place Eugene le Roy, Hautefort

…I noted it down straight away. What a treat that will be.

I know better than to arrive at any event in the Périgord at the time advertised. There is a recognised minimum *quart d'heure* delay for all events (and appointments, too; especially appointments). So I took the precaution of arriving at about twenty minutes past six. I parked my car near the entrance to the chateau a short distance away to give me convenient access to the gin and tonic I'd packed for the interval. I walked under the arch beneath the ramparts, dismayed though not entirely surprised to hear nothing and reached a spot where I stood overlooking the scene. A very few people occupied backless benches that had been arranged haphazardly in front of a rostrum on which two men were untangling cables by jumping them up and down, a procedure which, as you and I know, only tightens the knots and makes things more difficult. A proper bench, well-weathered but with a back to it, when turned round to face the square with help from a passing couple, made a comfortable vantage point and I settled myself down to watch the preparations.

A motley audience of jazz-lovers of all ages began to trickle in from above and behind, from left and right, from toddlers in nappies to the elderly; trickle, trickle. There was a lot of hand-shaking. On the dais microphones and amplifiers were manoeuvred into position.

Cables were plugged in and tripped over and plugged in again. One of the two men prepared his saxophone stand. Gosh – that's Dr Bob! Good gracious he's aged so you'd hardly recognise him. And put on weight. And the other one's the keyboard player. No sign of the others yet, though the drum kit's in place. There's not a lot of room left. Another man, who has been sitting on one of the front benches, struggles to his feet, shuffles shakily over to the stage and sets about tidying cables out of sight behind the ubiquitous black plastic apron front. He is helped up some wooden steps and on to the platform by both the men and over to a stool behind the drum kit. He is the drummer. The three of them start to test the equipment. Time goes by. Adjustments are made, jacks are re-located, amplifiers squeal, children scream, dogs bark. The man on the *clavier* starts up a rhythm and the guy on the *batterie* joins in for a bit. The saxophonist goes to his car. The others start without him. He returns with some more plastic sheeting and starts covering some of the important gear to protect against possible storm damage. The forecast is "set fair". He wipes his face with a piece of towel; he is exhausted; he takes up his instrument. They play a few bars. It is five past seven o'clock. They stop. The two help the third back down the difficult steps and they walk very, very slowly together across the road to the bar. Perhaps they are waiting for the fourth member to arrive. I will never know. It could be that they were in fact one of those *small* quartets that you have so often heard me joke about – "just the three of them". But I have left.

The Butler Did It

I have driven my gin and tonic home. Dave Brubeck is on the turntable. I listen. I drink. I stirred and I'm perhaps a little shaken. Disappointed, certainly; then later amused rather than cross. But if such a situation should arise again, I know what they (and I) can do.

§ § §

Each summer I pounce on the "Festivals" supplement stapled inside the June edition of "Vivre en Périgord". This magazine mainly serves to glorify the highness of one Bernard Cazeau, ex *maire* of Ribérac and currently Président du Conseil Général of the Dordogne. My neighbours play a game spotting the number of times his photograph appears each month. This time, hidden among the listings of concerts and exhibitions, between the pavement mime artists and the Purcell, the organ recitals and the flamenco, mention was made in very small print of Beatles in Jazz to be performed from 20.30 in the Grande Place at Jaure by a certain Fab Swing Trio as part of *Rencontres Artistiques* in the county of Grignols. Well, I'd never heard of Jaure, never heard of Grignols and the musicians' names meant nothing. But the map showed that the venue was only 30 minutes drive from Ribérac – so, worth a try. The worst that could happen would be that they turned out to be a "small trio – just the two of them". [Ironically, although all three did actually arrive and play, one of them was a late substitute.]

The contact number for information referred me to another contact number where I learned that the ticket price was 15 euros, the seats would be numbered and a buffet would be available from 19.30. Good. In fact, better than good.

We had no trouble finding Jaure but the *Place*, although *Grande* as in big, was just a large gravelled area and not what you'd call a *Place*. No edges. And *buffet*, even in French, was nowhere near a true description of what proved to be the catering arrangements. A bar had been set up to serve soft drinks in cans and beer *à la pression*. It would not have been fair of us to expect the beer to compare with the real ale we enjoyed recently during our travels through the Czech Republic (where Budweiser was originally created, incidentally). It was not going to impress – and didn't. I asked the man who was serving me (very, very slowly and with such concentration) if he could tell me where I might find the WC, anticipating the need for one later. He gave me the Gallic *haussement d'épaules* and suggested I put my question to a scruffy looking little man wearing a crumpled tee-shirt decorated with the American stars and stripes. "*Il sait tout!*" So I approached the fellow who'd been pointed out. "I'm told you know everything. Could you please direct me to the toilets?" And he very courteously did. "The reason you were told that I know everything is because I'm the mayor here. But, in fact, I know very little!". We shook hands and I went to share the information with Fanny. For the main culinary attraction *baguettes* had been cut into thirds then almost into halves lengthwise. A worried lady wiped a low-grade mustard on to one of the butterless halves with the back of a spoon.

Separately, a man was cooking extra-long sausages – choice of *merguez* or *anonyme* – on an improvised barbecue. These found their way one by one between the *baguette* halves. The length of time it had taken to accomplish this set the standard for the evening. You then handed over a paper token for which you had paid 2.5 euros at a trestle table a long way away and you could then do what you liked with the shape you were given wrapped in kitchen paper. Yummy. The time it took to consume this delicacy, which seemed to grow in the mouth, looked likely to make us late for the start of the music. But there was no need for concern because it became clear that the customary *quart d'heure périgordin* was going to be surpassed by a huge margin and a new benchmark established – to be re-christened *le doigt d'honneur dordognais*.

We went to locate our seats. Someone else had preferred ours to their own and the embarrassed lady who was directing us willed us not to make a fuss and of course we didn't. The chairs of moulded black plastic looked as though they were going to be unusually comfortable, certainly more so than the backless benches set out at the last open-air concert I'd gone to, but this was not to be, because mine "gave" as I leant back on it and I felt very insecure. Anyway, nearly everyone was seated by nine o'clock and even the organisers began to look fidgety. Still no sign of the musicians. A representative of the Grignols committee got to the microphone and seemed to assume that his explanation, that two of the musicians had become so delighted with the local cuisine that they were still eating in a local restaurant, made the late start acceptable. It was obvious he was making his speech last as long as he could. Then, relieved at seeing the mayor arrive to take his seat in the front row while still munching his sausage sandwich, he handed the microphone over to him *"pour quelques mots!"* The French love the sound of their own voice so to suggest "a *few* words" is laughable.

The substitute pianist arrived first and played on his own for a bit. He explained that Paul McCartney's compositions lent themselves to jazz treatment better than those of John Lennon or George Harrison, which was interesting. Eventually the well-fed unrepentant bass-player and drummer pitched up and felt the need to change out of their casual clothes and into even more casual clothes that might or might not have been cleaner. The concert got under way. They were excruciatingly awful. Darkness had come; it turned chilly and I went for the car rug. We waited politely for the interval before heading home. We didn't speak a lot.

The Butler Did It

Chapter Six
Lest we forget…

THERE IS STILL WORK TO do.

This winter I've been trying my hand at plastering between the niches in the walls of the gallery bedroom. Having been tipped off about French plaster, I specifically asked the builders' merchant for slow-setting plaster and was told I would have 48 (not 47 or 49 but 48) minutes to play (*play?!*) with once it was mixed. This was confirmed on the printed outer. The instructions also recommended letting the mixture stand for 6 minutes. Which I did. Twenty minutes later I was still trying to chip the rock solid plaster from the container. I imagine it would be impossible to attempt in summer temperatures.

Slightly confused, not to say humiliated by this embarrassing initiation into the pitfalls of this, the messiest of all the skills required in the business of building, I contacted my technical adviser in England. Equally humiliating, he showed no surprise. After such observations as "Should really only be tackled by a younger man" and "You oughta 'ave a second bloke to do yer mixin' ", he suggested my chances of success might be improved by first applying a cement render and following that up in due course with a thin coat of a very sloppy plaster mix. One can begin to see how this came to inspire scenes for pantomime.

Thus encouraged, I followed his advice most diligently and I can now assure you that my efforts at rendering bear a close comparison with those of my plastering when measured in terms of the amount of waste. This is due less to problems of quick setting and more to gravitational forces. I've adapted a well-known proverb to read: "Neither plasterer nor renderer be."

Each morning, now, my first task is to mix a small quantity of mortar, talking to it nicely all the while and then coercing it to stick to, not slide down, a small area of wall. This way, by not being too ambitious, some 60 square inches of it (or approximately 375 square centimetres to sound more impressive), obediently adheres to roughly where I'm targeting. To help you visualise this statistic: 60 sq.ins. equates to about half the size of a medium to small breadboard which, as a size in its own right, I've always thought of as handy, *never* imagining that it would one day serve as a means of measuring my prowess at rendering; as in: "I did almost 3-and-a-half bread-boards yesterday, but only 2 today".

If I step back to assess the result and betray even the slightest glimmer of satisfaction, the mortar resents such presumption, takes umbrage, turns Bolshie and heads southwards. On the bright side, the benefit from this is that, however pessimistically small an amount I prepare, there is always a substantial quantity left over on the floor to use on the myriad of filling and making-good jobs that came with the property.

I reached the point when the day arrived for the last half bread-board's worth of rendering. I climbed to the now familiar position – it has been in my dreams the last few nights – and sprayed a small amount of clean water over the surface text-book style…I think it's going to work…it's sticking…if I go a bit higher that'll finish it off…there's enough on the hawk (that's the name the professionals call the bread-board)…the building seems to be holding its breath… go for it! Ye-e-e-e-es! Red Letter Day!

I was halfway down the ladder when I heard it – the unmistakable dull thud of cement as it beat me to the ground floor. I used my new rude word: "Oh! *Mercredi!*" But it was undeniably my own fault. In the excitement I'd neglected to talk to it nicely. Or, indeed, at all. Oh well, same time tomorrow.

The sloppy plastering stage is scheduled for some time in the Spring – just to keep it nice and vague – when I should be feeling more, well, positive. This is, after all, a designated stress-free zone.

§ § §

EDF, until recently, have been unexpectedly – and most probably unintentionally – accommodating. The *compteur de chantier* (building-site electrical supply terminal) which they installed for a 12 month limited period is still my conduit for power nearly 3 years later. The original ground-worker had taken responsibility for payment and with the invoices going directly to him I'd no way of knowing how large my debt was getting. I wrote to him 18 months ago requesting copies so that I could refund him the money. I thought he would be pleased to hear from me but there was no reply. A copy by registered letter had the same result.

Then about a month ago he was on the 'phone wanting to see me urgently. Two days later he arrived bearing paperwork. After the initial (electric) shock we agreed on a plan. I made out three enormous cheques to be banked a month apart and he went off happy.

Thursday lunchtime he was on the phone again "I have to tell you EDF will remove your terminal on Monday." What?!! At any time during the last two years they could have decided *un oeuf* is *un oeuf* and given me a month's notice of termination. There is still a lot to do. The house-wiring is complete but has yet to be inspected and 65 metres of domestic mains cable is still in a coil in the barn. I involved my local mayor and he got me a *week's* reprieve. Why all this sudden hurry? Maybe someone in the Montignac office is in trouble because of the oversight. Hurrying now won't change anything.

Two strong young men from my electrician's team arrived on Friday morning to insert the cable through the underground tubing buried in the driveway all that time ago. After a certain distance it wouldn't budge. In their opinion, the heavy goods lorries, that have been delivering all manner of materials during the period, have squashed the tubing flat. Another long trench seems the only solution; more expense and a new scar on the hillside. Who, I wonder, will have the last laugh?

Here is a clue: one of the electricians had needed to isolate the current and hadn't turned back on all the switches. That evening I stepped into an ice-cold bath.

Next day. My electrician is a good egg – he's got his chaps here on a Saturday morning to dig an experimental hole where they think the blockage is located. Mid-morning and the obstruction *has* been found. By lunchtime the mains cable has made it from the meter in the barn to the *disjoncteur* in the kitchen ready for connection on Monday. That's the good news; but the bad news is that the other tube running parallel is too *écrasé* to be used for the telephone connection. One thing at a time.

9th December. The inspector from Le Consuel, EDF Limoges is due. It is his signature on the pass certificate that I need for the *branchement definitif.* The team has been here all week double-checking their work and their boss is here to smooth things along. All goes well except that a very expensive light-fitting for the bathroom, supplied with a transformer for safety reasons, no longer meets with new regulations that came in last June just a few weeks after I bought it. However the chief electrician arranges by his *portable* for one of his chaps to replace it next day and the inspector goes away satisfied. The *certificat de conformité* will be in the post direct to my electrician's home address because he also needs to sign it before it is physically in the hands of the EDF Operations Centre. Mains connection will just beat the deadline on the 15th for disconnection of the building site supply. I left happily for the evening jazz concert and on to the weekend *chez* Fanny.

I returned to base on Sunday evening to find no electricity. With temperatures dropping I had taken the precaution of jacking up the heating and assumed that the switches must have tripped. Not so. The white *compteur de chantier* was easy to find in the moonlight but dangling from it was the disconnected cable. The b*gg*rs had come without warning on Friday afternoon and cut me off without making the new connection. It's freezing.

Monday morning and my neighbours had kindly charged my mobile 'phone overnight so I was able to contact my really patient electrician. He received the *"consuel"* in Saturday's post and, confirming the change of the bathroom light fitting, signed it and put it in the collection box on Sunday afternoon. His advice to me is to go to La Poste, where his envelope still is, he has checked, identify myself, retrieve it and then drive up to Limoges with it, find the inspector's office, obtain the final document and drive with that back down to the EDF H.Q. at Montignac. And to lose no time…

It is afternoon by the time I reach the waiting-room. I'm all prepared to charm the socks off the receptionist when I am faced with a beautiful young *man*, glossy dark wavy hair, very polite. His name is Vincent and he displays outwardly a great deal of efficiency and sympathy. He takes the precious piece of paper to his colleagues who are less cooperative, unpleasant even. The first date I am offered is the 28th! I go into overdrive and find myself quoting French law, the Treaty of Rome, Human Rights, freezing pipes, thawing freezer (I don't actually possess one) and the fact that I'm approaching my 104th birthday. It hurts that they accept my exaggerated age without question.

After another long wait one of them gets through to the *Urgence Rouge* office and thanks to his instrument being switched to loud-speaker I can hear the badinage and derisive laughter of his colleagues as they ignore the earnestness of my case. The offer this time is the 20th. I make it clear to him that I'm not going to leave until he matches the original date of the 15th. It is now turned 3p.m. He is on to his chief who has just returned from lunch. He agrees to come himself (!) sometime during Wednesday morning, he cannot say exactly when. [I learned later that there is a statute saying that they are obliged to make a connection within 48 hours of receiving the official certificate. I wish I'd known that at the time.] I leave elated and then realise I have still two freezing nights to endure.

Wednesday the 15th. Last night was not so bad as Margot had filled and thrust two hot-water bottles at me as I left the warmth of their fire yesterday evening.

Midday has come and gone and I feel obliged once more to call on the help of my long-suffering electrician. He rings me back mid-afternoon. "Don't leave; stay there, someone *will* come."

Darkness falls. 6.10p.m. A car draws up and the lovely young Vincent appears with a torch and a tool-box! He has been instructed by his boss to come at the *end* of his shift. Once again he is most polite, explaining staff shortages as the cause of the problem. EDF

The Butler Did It

is a much despised company so with the inevitable low morale it is no wonder that they can't recruit *and keep* enough people.

It was a huge relief to have the power back on and I rushed round clicking the heating switches and the hot-water controls. And what was that about a celebratory tincture?

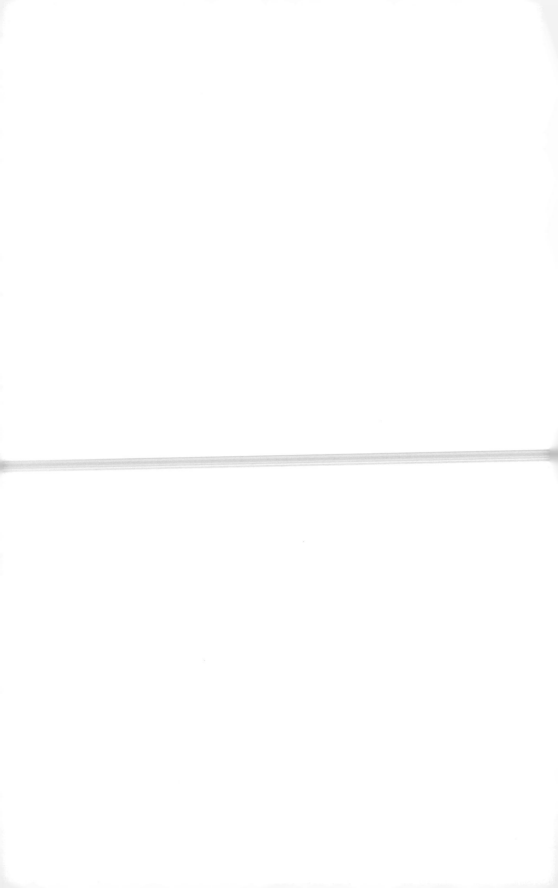

Chapter Seven
A Postcard from Northern Portugal

WE HAD A GREAT TOUR, leaving France by the western end of the Pyrénées and continuing along the Atlantic coast, then keeping to the Bilbao road to arrive at our first outbound (and our last homebound) overnight stop. If you haven't been you should definitely go. The Guggenheim Museum is the principal attraction, of course, but there are others, including in particular the atmospheric Café Boulevard (for the best continental breakfast I've had anywhere), full of Art Deco touches to the lighting and décor plus free tango lessons upstairs; and in common with most Spanish towns there is an area in the Caseo Viejo known as the Barrio Humido (the "Wet Quarter") – because of the quantity of liquid sloshing around. But maybe you know all this already. Our short stay coincided with Bilbao Atlètico *versus* Réal Madrid and the 2-1 victory resulted in *una noche sin sueno.*

The Guggenheim

In spite of that we took the exciting route in the morning, round the hairpin bends of the picturesque mountains (which echoed with Fanny's screams) and the breathtaking lakes of los Picos de l'Europa to reach Léon, a nightmare of a place not helped by impossible-to-follow directions supplied by the hotel receptionist who had obviously never driven in this city riddled with one-way streets, dead-ends and *entradas prohibidas.* To exacerbate her already fragile mood – Fanny, in a strop, had caught her thumb slamming the car door – we got trapped in the underground car park. Once we had calmed down, it was pleasant enough to stroll around the Plaza de San Martin and the cathedral precincts.

Then, next day, we headed for Bragança, stopping to lunch in the *castillo* of a very pretty village on a hill above the main road called Puebla de Sanabria before crossing the Portuguese border and the Parque Natural de Montesinho described by some as austere but we preferred to think of as unspoilt. We were welcomed warmly at the charming small hotel by the slightly puzzled *duena*. We thought nothing of it and retired early.

After a good night's sleep we descended hungrily to the *comedor* but there was no sign of anybody. We'd made an effort to be first and expected everything to be in place. Some time later there were noises followed by appetising smells from the *cocina* and we tucked in to breakfast.

The Dukes of Bragança featured prominently in Portugal's history, reigning over both Portugal (1640-1910) and Brazil (1822-1899). We could hardly leave without having a look around the medieval part of this one-time important fortified city and climbed up to the ramparts in the hope of seeing the view from what was left of the castle. Once again there was nobody there. We decided to wait and were eventually let in by a surprised-looking official. It had been worth the wait; the views from the top of the keep were splendid.

It wasn't till we stopped for what our tummies told us was time to eat that we realised we should have adjusted our watches when we crossed the border – Lisbon time is Greenwich time!

On we drove to Chaves, the Portuguese word for "keys", named when the town was built as a fortified lookout on the banks of the

Tamega facing Spain. It was fortified again today as we circled the outskirts trying unsuccessfully to penetrate the barriers set up for a cycle race. There was no shortage of police patrol cars but no way of reaching our hotel. We were told we would have to be patient and wait. But we were well placed when the event was over. They were so helpful and guided us to the entrance of the street we wanted. Then two of the *policia* lifted the barrier out of the way and gestured us

Castillo de
Sanabria

through. Uncompleted road-works lead-ing to the hotel were full of sharp ridges and débris and I was concerned for the tyres. We found a way in to the hotel and I had to trek round the corridors

The Butler Did It

to find a receptionist. Then we unloaded the bags; then we asked the way to the secure parking. It was in another part of town. Reversing back down the way we came, wincing with every shock to the tyres, we arrived to where the *policia* had tidily replaced the *barrera*. I heaved it out of the way and we soon found the multi-storey parking. But the entry bar was locked down; no call for parking on a Sunday, it seems. Plenty of cars visible

Bragança – castle ramparts

inside, though. They must have their own pass-code. Hullo – a car driving out. The driver stopped and pointed to a telephone number and about half an hour later in response to our call a very pleasant young man arrived full of apologies from the proprietor, his father. He indicated where we should park and then proposed taking us on a guided tour of the whole town, of which he sounded really proud. He told us he'd studied at Lisbon University but once he'd obtained his law degree he was back in Chaves like a shot. The tour included the thermal springs. He also recommended some eating places but in the end the best compensation for all the difficulties was the lovely restaurant we discovered for ourselves in a side street. It was jam-packed with locals – always a good sign – and we enjoyed an excellent *jantar* with a beautiful *reserva*.

§ § §

We moved on to Vila Real, recommended by Natalie and Brigitte, owners of the 'La Hacienda' Bar in Terrasson, who hail from here. Described as a tiny city, presumably on the basis that it only has a tiny cathedral, it is a really lively "university town" in atmosphere. The balcony of our third floor room gave us views of the *centro cuidad* with its bright lights and dancing fountains from the early evening onwards, views below to the bus station yard that operated from beneath the hotel starting at 6 a.m. and views above to the flight-path of the nearby airport. I really wouldn't want to be here at peak season but it was by no means crowded in September and the weather was exceptionally good. What was more, once we walked into town, there was a *pastelaria* (pastry shop) every few metres! [Unfortunately, as it turned out, because they proved to be an addiction from which Fanny never recovered.]

It was from Vila Real that we set out on two excursions by car.

Léon
Cathedral

The Butler Did It

Mateus
Manor

Los
Picos de
l'Europa

The first was to fulfil a long-felt want to visit the Douro Valley during the *cosecha* and sample the famous port; and the second was also *vino*-related – a shorter drive to Mateus Manor, the *palaço* instantly recognisable from the distinctive label on the gourd-shaped bottle of Mateus Rosé, a very popular wine in England in the '50s.

Up to this point we had kept to our planned route, but on the way to Amarante, eventual destination Guimaraes, I took a left turn at random into hilly rugged country and the back of beyond. We stopped at the end of a village where we ran out of road. No sound; no movement. But picturesque barns and partly collapsed buildings enticed us from the car to take photographs. A woman all in black appeared from nowhere carrying flowers, gave us a smile, said *"Bom dia!"* and continued on her way to the cemetery. I busied myself with arty shots of tobacco-leaf drying sheds and a wonderful boat-shaped cart and Fanny walked back through the

Tiny cathedral at Vila Real

deserted hamlet. When I looked up to see where she'd got to, she was talking to a woman in an unusually friendly and animated manner and in no time at all we were invited into one of the houses, which we had supposed to be uninhabited, to meet her husband. They lived off the land and, it was clear, had very little. We were very touched when they made us sit down to a piece of cake and a glass of wine. Their only son had gone to France to work on a building site but was stricken with leukemia suddenly and was now in hospital in Paris. They were *so* worried and wanted to talk. They both spoke French, having lived there at some period in their lives, and Fanny's words of sympathy were so well-chosen that they asked if she would kindly speak to their son if they got through to him on the 'phone. Which is

The Douro Valley

what happened. And we left, feeling very choked, but pleased that we had made the spontaneous diversion that had led to such a moving experience.

§ § §

Amarante was worth the short stop. The St.Gonsalo Bridge, high above the Tamega, leads to the imposing monastic church in Italian Renaissance style dedicated to the same saint. Gonsalo was a 13th century hermit and became the patron saint of marriage, which makes you stop and think.

There is much to attract the visitor in Guimaraes: the palace built in 1401 by Alfonso I, first Duke of Bragança is now a museum, like many others; the *Igreja Sao Miguel do Castelo*, a 12th century Romanesque church; the *Igreja Nossa Senhora de Oliveira*; the *Paços do Concelho*, etc.,etc. Plus an impressive castle with seven towers round the keep. Apparently. We saw none of these. We did walk the length of the *rua de Santa Maria* where 14th and 15th century houses, typically with wrought iron grilles and granite cornices, lead the way to the old quarter. But we had parked the car quite a distance away in an area with lots of shifty looking characters and I was ill at ease. So we made for our overnight accommodation. This was a sumptuous villa inside a gated park belonging to the once-upon-a-time butler to the Portuguese Ambassador to Switzerland! Didn't *he* do well! The interior matched the grandeur of the outside. The reception area was huge with groups of settees and low tables with lamps and soft furnishings to rival Claridge's or The Savoy! The owner and his wife greeted us in

great style and after refreshment we were shown to our simple but luxuriously accessorised bedroom suite. Supper was served to us on the terrace as it was such a very pleasantly warm evening and for breakfast next day it was one course after another. Perfect.

[I should like to go back to Guimaraes for a proper appreciation of the town but also to drive up to *Bom Jésus do Monte* east of Braga which we somehow managed to miss. Actually, you have the choice of

driving up, taking the funicular or walking up one of the elaborately sculpted stone staircases, which is what the pilgrims do; on their knees. Apparently, a fine vista awaits you as well as a fountain and other water features. I kick myself when I think how close we were and didn't stop.]

Valença do Minho old town is an unusual double city consisting of two fortresses (irregular polygons) linked by a single-width bridge and a vaulted passage. Our hotel was situated furthest from the extremely off-putting military style entrance but we found our way, once again, with help from a friendly police escort. *Inside* the walls it was a dream. Spain has its *paradores*; in Portugal there are the *pousadas*. I had so enjoyed the Spanish experience in the early 80s and was dying to make the comparison. I was not disappointed. In fact the Portuguese welcome was many degrees warmer than that in Spain. We were the only guests in the dining room that evening which made it particularly special. Our bedroom had views to Spain over the Minho river which forms the northern limit of the country. Beyond that is the pilgrims' trail to Santiago de Compostela, not on our itinerary.

§ § §

The St Gonsalo Bridge at Amarante

The monastery church

During our travels in this largely unspoilt part of Portugal (in total contrast to the Algarve), we had sampled four or five of the "hundred ways with cod" for which the Portuguese are supposedly renowned; had some memorable encounters with lovely people, fellow-travellers as well as Portuguese; and returned home eventually with just a few bottles of previously untried excellent wine and enough photos to fill an entire album.

Our route back over the Minho into Spain took us eastwards and then south to the planned nightstop at Paredes de Nava in the

The Butler Did It

Province of Palencia. It was a depressing dump of a town and when we located the address we also found that the house immediately next door was a pile of rubble, having completely collapsed. When we rang the bell, we heard footsteps inside scurrying away. It was an easy decision to press on to the capital, Palencia, where we were so grateful to find accommodation in a boring old modern 4-star hotel. Thence north-north-west to our last stop, Bilbao, to check into the same sister-and-brother run hotel but there was a mix-up over the booking and next morning, a dispute over the bill. On top of which, the breakfast we had anticipated enjoying at the Café Boulevard was not available: "Closed on Sunday"! It was never more obviously time to go home.

Pousada do Poco de Valenca

View across the Minho to Spain

Audiobituary

On the 6th October 2006 at the age of 15 years and 194,607 miles and on the D706 at the edge of Campagne, a tiny village between Le Bugue and Les Eyzies, the 2-litre Audi '80' registration number 8608 TZ 24, *née* J157 XHO, came to rest.

It was clear she was in pain as she struggled up the steep incline from Siorac du Périgord and the whine developed into a growling plea for mercy just as gravity took over at the summit and propelled her headlong round the scary hairpin bends with nowhere to go but onwards while the momentum lasted, reaching the T-junction at the Route de la Préhistoire and the unrealistically optimistic "STOP" sign. Something imploded spectacularly in the region of her bowels as she gave a final shudder on the verge. On the verge of what? Best not to contemplate. It wasn't the peaceful end you would have chosen – but it was quick.

She had led a charmed life. Firstly in a relationship with a genteel lady owner who treated her with kindness, regular services and a good deal of polish. Secondly in the hands of an adventurer who introduced her to foreign travel and a life full of the unexpected where appearances counted less and love was not measured in car-washes.

In return she had given him impeccable service ever since leaving England and most particularly during their search in September of the millenium year for a property to share in *la France profonde*. The new liaison flourished; they were seen everywhere together. Recently, however, she had become a little capricious, at times temperamental, possibly in reaction to his increasingly unviable demands and as is so often the case the partnership came to the end of the road.

She leaves a trailer and two warning triangles.

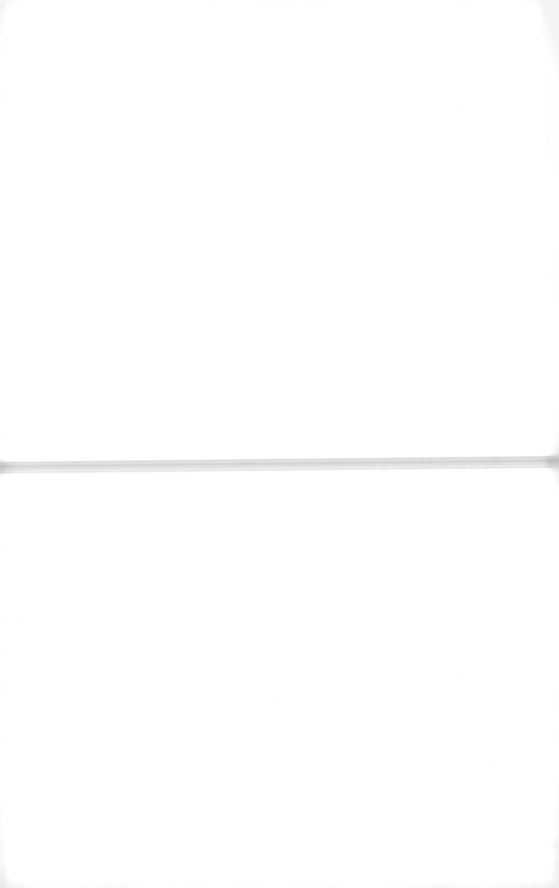

Chapter Eight
Lest We Forget...
this is still a building site

Le Cirque du Beau Soleil

IN BETWEEN THE RUMBLE OF engines and the rattle of tiles there can be heard the sound of whistling as a troupe of happy jugglers, acrobats and highly wired performers posing as *couvreurs* (roofers) as well as the odd clown, set about dismantling my *toiture*. M. Serge Bambou and his team arrived at 8a.m. from the other side of Terrasson and were soon lifting and sorting for re-use the original hand-made tiles. The rejects shatter as they land on the heap of débris that'll be the hardcore for the new terrace. The rest are stacked on the old laths. The ridge tiles will not be re-used. Down the hill comes the Manitou with its telescopic arm carrying an empty wooden crate to which the sound tiles are being transferred by a human chain throwing them two, three, sometimes four at a time to the man on the cradle until it is full. Then it is lowered to the ground and the process repeated. Meanwhile, another guy is chopping out the old pointing between the tower and the main roof and around the chimney stack. Occasionally the boss will call instructions but mostly they are silent, apart from the whistling and the hammering.

Serge Bambou is proud of his family name. Back in the 1800s Franciscan monks in this region acted as itinerant social workers and it was customary for those orphans in their care who had no known identity to be named after trees. Serge's ancestor became Bambou.

As fast as the old *lattes* are being removed from one side, one of the chaps is unrolling the insulation (TRI ISO 9 – a modern foil-covered 2cms. thick substitute for 20cms. category Rockwool) and stapling it on to the *charpente* – the timber frame from which we get the word 'carpenter'. I invested in the insulation when it was on promotion and had it in stock. It has served me well: the reason why the date for the work has been brought forward is because it would have been a mistake to delay until the summer when the likelihood of the sun's glare reflecting off the shiny surface would have made it impossible to handle, even with sunglasses. I've been jumped up the long queue of customers.

I went round to see what was happening on the other side. Two men were bouncing their way confidently along loose planks laid on metal brackets cantilevered under the eaves. Probably conforming to a European directive, France has begun to be more health-and-safety conscious and building-site practices such as these are becoming rarer. However dexterous these men are – and however appropriately in keeping with my circus theme they may be – these stunts will be illegal by the end of the year.

Prior to the re-roofing, my *menuisier* had erected a full length porch-like framework on the terrace side of the house . To avoid this looking like an afterthought and to give a more authentic look to the traditional Périgordine style I'm trying to keep, the roofer has recommended changing the angle of slope of the chevrons. I have seen the good sense in this but I will be left with the problem of building up the end wall to fill the tapering space between the new roof line and the original. A roofer's job description does not include masonry. I'll have to get hold of some scaffolding if I'm to do it myself. But for the moment it's the sacred hour of twelve o'clock. With all the chevrons now in place – as well as the *coyaux*, the short lengths that form the distinctive change in the outline of the roof – they are away to the Estaminet in Badefols d'Ans where I've arranged for them to have lunch.

Back to work and there's the buzz of chain-saws as new laths are trimmed to length and then nailed in place. It is taking longer on this side because the insulation is hiding the original chevrons, comprised of irregular tree trunks for the most part and there seems to be more miss than hit. I've stopped watching.

As three of the men are doing the final hammering of the day, two others are re-tiling the far edge and perching stacks of tiles ready for tomorrow. It is really all coming together. They didn't pack up until 7p.m.

§ § §

Back early again next day with crates of re-cycled well-matched hand-made tiles to replace the discards, the team was running like clockwork. By 11a.m. with the end of the work in sight, the Manitou descended with the last crate's worth of tiles and sank one of its feet right through the lid of the *fosse septique*. This poor tank must be jinxed; it was clear from the very start that it didn't really like it here. Anyway, in no time at all, cement had been mixed and shuttering to the right size had been built and before my eyes a replacement concrete lid was hardening. No problems, only solutions. And the rain waited until they left. Pretty satisfactory. There's only one thing better than seeing workmen arriving and that is seeing them leaving.

§ § §

The following Friday afternoon. I had started to think about how to put this "long porch" to best use. Log storage, certainly. A freezer wouldn't be a bad idea. Perhaps some hooks for odds and ends. I looked up at the overhead supports and thought I noticed a crack where they had been mortared into the wall of the house. I looked more closely and there was a centimetre gap. "By gum!" I said to myself, "it's all starting to move!" Nightmare. *"Le toit qui bouge!"*

I jumped to the telephone to contact the joiner who came over *tout de suite.* "You're right" he said. "You'd better get on to your roofer. I'll wait." I rang the roofer. "I've got the joiner here. He says I'm right – the roof's moving!"

I have to hand it to them. There was no discussion as to where the blame lay. They spoke together on the 'phone and arranged to meet here early tomorrow morning – Saturday. A sign they were seriously worried.

§ § §

They worked together all day. They had brought everything necessary: blocks and tackle, carabiners, rope, bolts, drills, metal straps of different lengths and widths, wooden splints and tools. They dealt with it in a very serious and professional way. It would be easy to say that it should never have happened and it probably wouldn't have if they had each been aware of the specification used on both sides of the job. But I prefer to remember the episode (not really a chapter) as one where two people reacted properly to an emergency, behaved responsibly and effectively and averted a disaster. I'd like a little recognition for spotting it so soon. But that was sheer luck.

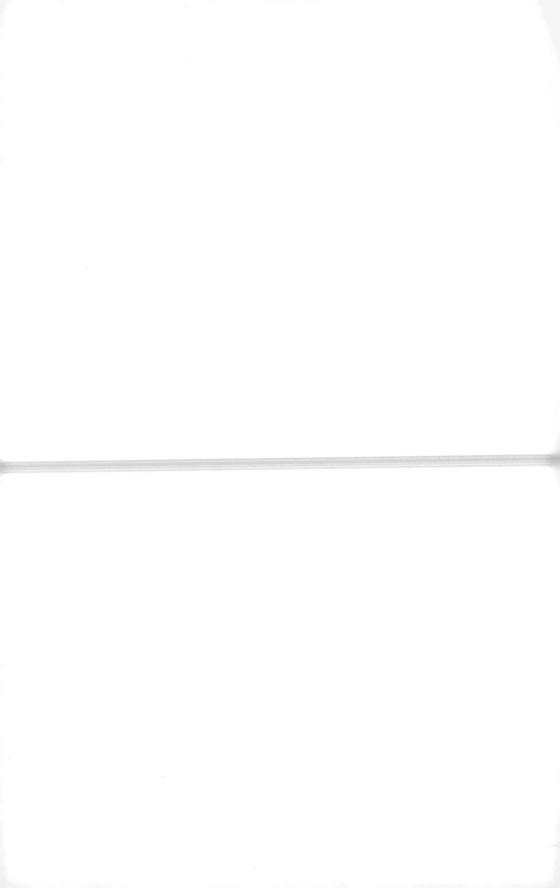

Chapter Nine
Sting Where is Thy Death?

EARLY AUTUMN 2008. TODAY SAW an unwelcome addition to the already over-crowded corner of my brain that is sign-posted 'French vocabulary' – *'frelon'*, meaning hornet. *'Nid'* (nest) was already there.

The *'ramoneur'* (chimney sweep) turned up inconveniently at lunchtime, running late by several days. I was so pleased to see him I insisted he went ahead with it. He set about the task and hit a snag almost straightaway. It suddenly became clear why, back in late April when the need of the wood-burning stove was coming to an end, it had been noticeably difficult to get the fire going. The *'blocage'* (blockage) had been caused by the sneaky invasion of an extended family of New Age hornets camping in the *'conduit'* (flue). And the little *'salauds'*, or *'mendiants'* (b*gg*rs) if you want to be polite, must have been squatting there all summer.

If I'd been more attentive to the faint "fly-trapped-in-a-bottle" back-ground hum I might have dealt with them sooner but there are so many strange sounds in this house that I have been forced to accept that I am not the sole occupant in spite of what I claimed in the recent *'recensement'* (census). Anyway, I chose to ignore it like I do the rest.

The *'ramoneur'* poked around nervously for a bit which the hornets didn't like very much and as they spilled resentfully out of the stove and into the room he swatted at a few of them unsuccessfully with my *'tapette'* (much prettier than fly-swat). Having stirred things up he left, recommending that I waited until the *'frénésie'* (frenzy – I hope you're finding these translations helpful) had quietened down before lighting some newspaper in the stove to test if the flue was now sufficiently unblocked to make a fire possible in order to smoke them out.

The second I opened the stove door I was stung. In the middle finger. This is the one used as a *'geste'* (gesture) by French drivers to express extreme displeasure. The idea of smoking out my intruders was abandoned for the time being but not the idea of the gesture as I still had my other middle finger in working order. I was surprised at how good this made me feel.

I am hardly what you would call a country boy, certainly not up to snuff when it comes to matters of Nature. Word had reached me, though, from more than one source along the lane that a hornet's sting frequently had quite fatal results. Very fatal, sometimes! Also, this year, there was the front-page news item announcing that Chinese hornets have landed in Europe and that they are, not too surprisingly, more efficient than the local species, knocking minutes off the time it takes for you to die, once stung.

Chinese (or Asian) Hornet

I decided that the nationality of the ones domiciled in my chimney was only academic. There had been no verbal exchange in the moments before I slew the one that attacked me nor anything about his eyes to betray his country of origin. He had been reluctant to die – something that we had in common. It was time I telephoned my 'généraliste' (G.P.). It was now 2.15p.m.

I had the feeling I'd got him out of bed. Considering that it is a bit of a lottery deciding who to choose as your doctor, who in the French system you are obliged to choose and name, I had felt lucky to have chanced on a good one based entirely on his being the nearest. The bonus was that he was normally cheerful. But not this time. I quickly summarised the events culminating in the skin puncture. He seemed full of unconcern. Was I allergic to hornet stings, he eventually enquired? "Who could say?" I replied, "but if I come quickly to your surgery perhaps, together, we could find out."

He asked me if I was having trouble with my breathing and I assured him that what he could hear was just the normal France Telecom interference on the line. There was another pause. He said that, if I liked, it would be O.K. for me to come to his 'cabinet' (!) in about three hours' time, say 6p.m. I said I could be dead by then. "5.30, *alors. A tout à l'heure.*"

I 'phoned Fanny, at her office. "Dab some alcohol on it" was her advice, knowing full well that there is always alcohol in the house and that I may be willing to spare a few drops in extreme medical necessity. If not, I was to feel free to splash on some of her Coco Chanel. In the end I found a long-forgotten complimentary sample phial of after-shave in the back of the bathroom surgery, sorry, cabinet. Then, tightening an elastic band at the finger's base as an improvised 'garrot' (tourniquet – you'd expect tourniquet to be French, wouldn't you , but it's not – well it is but it means turnstile or sprinkler) to stop the poison spreading into the bloodstream,

The Butler Did It

I sucked on the place where the skin had been stung, applied the freebie antiseptic and poured myself a sharpener from the drinks cupboard, 1 part brandy to 1 part brandy.

Actually, I began to feel rather foolish because, it seemed, I wasn't actually dying after all. How reliable is all this hearsay information? Sting where is thy death?! So at 5.30 I phoned to cancel the appointment. You've to pay the doctor on the spot here as I'm sure I've mentioned before; better to put the money towards the pest controller's bill.

§ § §

Postscript: Monsieur Olivier Gaillard (the appropriately named 'Ollie the Brave'), the '*disinfestation*' specialist from Les Pages Jaunes, cannot make it for another four days. He is '*débordé*' (snowed under). At this time of year the extermination business is extremely brisk and he is doing very well indeed.

So, ALL TOGETHER now:
"'Tis the season to be Ollie,
FA LA LA LA LA, FA LA LA LA!"

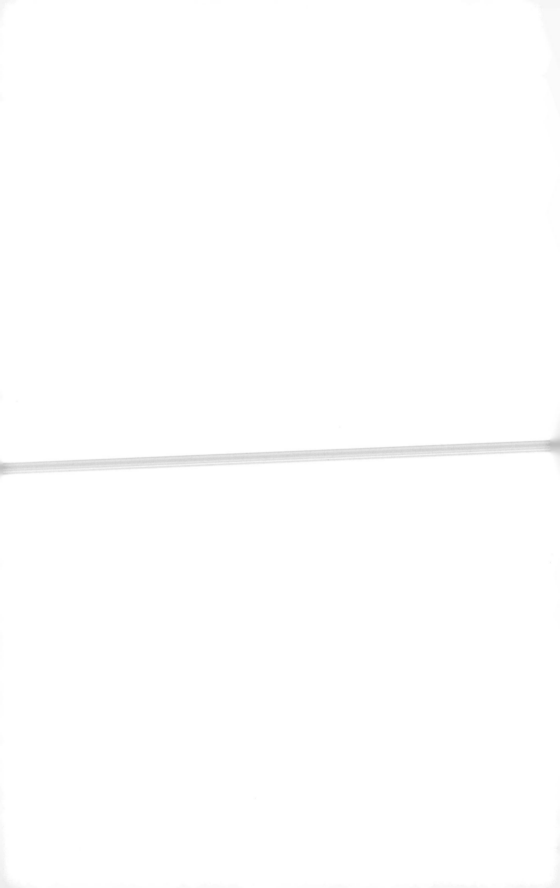

Chapter Ten
A Whistle-stop Tour round Central European Capitals

(with more history than geography and not too much of either.)

NOEL COWARD HAS ONE OF his characters say, when describing his travels: "Very big, China. And Japan? very small." Succinct. Not an adjective you could apply to these jottings but he and I share the same aim. To entertain. If you're only interested in facts (and there are a few included), I believe you'll be able to find plenty of those on something called "Google".

I have only once before been seen in a charabanc, during a life-span that now exceeds the biblical three-score-years-and-ten and I'm not saying by how much, and here I am about to spend 11 days in one. Fanny and I are fulfilling an ambition to reach parts of Europe that we'd never reached before and without the stress of finding the way and somewhere to park the car when we get there. She will never let me forget Léon.

We have driven under cover of darkness to the outskirts of Brantôme, the self-styled 'Venice of the Périgord' to board a coach at the inconspicuous headquarters of a recommended tour operator. At 0530 in the capable, we hope, hands of Serge the Néanderthal driver and with Ophélie as our pretty young *accompagnatrice*, we have left the depot and during the two hours that follow, involving many stops, the vehicle slowly, very slowly, fills with wrinklies, some in regrettable shorts displaying an assortment of varicose features, others on metal crutches (called *cannes anglaises* for some obscure reason), some with hearing aids and others with knee operation scars or goozles not yet removed; a very mixed bag. Let me introduce you to a few who we got to know or be aware of.

In the seats immediately in front of us and well-placed for the on-board toilet and the door for hasty exits, are a fidgety couple with squeaky voices and, as it turned out, weak bladders. Then on the left of the aisle and two rows up is an intellectual pair who have insisted on speaking to me in very "'Allo, Allo'" English on subjects such as French philosophers, Jane Austen and the choral work of Schubert. [Fanny hit that on the head straightaway – "We're not interested in any of that!"] The chap in the seat behind was very "under thumb"; his other half was very scornful when, in the course of our progress through the different countries, hotels had to be telephoned with the request to forward what he'd left behind. I liked him a lot. Other couples you would never have paired by their looks – not in the proverbial million years – though I suppose you could say the same of us really. One little chap, very deaf, proclaimed loudly for all to hear how proud he was of his wife who, returning slowly and understandably reluctantly to the coach after one of the many comfort stops, had paused to embrace with open arms a shower of rain (the only one on the whole trip, as it happened). This company knows who it is catering for. Misfits sums it up. I found another couple, he over-weight in a very inappropriate as well as grubby safari suit and she with an unusual pair of mis-matched eyes that made you unsure of whether she was looking at you or at someone over your shoulder, rather patronising. I overheard him saying to her (about me) "*Il joue un rôle.*" I don't like to think I'm so obvious. I was the only non-French traveller and as far as I could eventually make out, the only one not on medication.

Attempts to doze off were interrupted either by sporadic recitals of facts by way of commentary from our courier or by the sudden and aggressive crushing of empty plastic water bottles. Why do people do that?

§ § §

The first overnight stop was at Ostwald near Strasbourg. It was thoughtful of the Company to provide us with a lot of descriptive and historical information about this place because we didn't actually get to see it [or Strasbourg.]. Named by Irish missionaries after an Anglo-Saxon King who became a saint, the unfortunate village suffered plague and pestilence and centuries of crises and destitution, perhaps as some kind of reprisal. In any case it didn't augur well for us. The driver took three goes before he found the hotel partially hidden in a Commercial Zone behind a Leroy Merlin and a branch of FoirFouille. It went very quiet when he manoeuvred to park alongside an Ibis Budget; there was no rush to descend from the bus.

Later. I had just started picking experimentally at a plate of steamed fish and *choucroute* – which did little to endorse Ibis' "renown in the world of cuisine" – when we were assailed by a deafening alarm. Minutes went by. It was not something you could ignore but nobody was doing anything. Everybody looked at everybody else. The waiters continued waiting. It seemed there was nobody in charge. I went out to the reception area to see what could be switched off. The noise was coming from an overhead alarm. Still nobody about. I pulled a chair over and stood on it to unscrew the cover. The noise was dreadful. There were no visible wires to disconnect, no contacts to be seen. I found something on the counter to hit it with. It worked; the noise stopped. I replaced the chair, left the cover on the counter and continued to the door marked *'Toilettes'*. By the time I returned to the dining room calm was restored. I said to the driver "The inmates of France's prisons ate better than we did tonight." He replied that complaints had been noted and would be reported but the manager had gone off duty.

An inauspicious start.

§ § §

By mid-morning the next day we had crossed the German border and were bowling along the *autobahn* towards the Bavarian city of **Nüremberg**. At the centre of one of the principal industrial regions of southern Germany, its wealth deriving originally from the goldsmiths, then the bronze foundries and more recently the manufacture of machine tools, electrical equipment and toys, it was a relief to find ourselves inside the walls of the very picturesque and photogenic medieval town. The Kaiserberg, seat of kings and emperors, dominates the ramparts. It's all too pristine to be original. That's because in January 1945 ninety percent of the city centre was bombed out by Allied aircraft. A fact too many but an amazing restoration.

On the way to lunch I dived into the Albrecht Dürer-Haus, now a museum. Dürer isn't everybody's cup of tea; his copperplate engravings, for which he is probably best known, are amazingly detailed but a bit grim, I find, the anatomical drawings undoubtedly skilful but somewhat, well, grotesque. However his actual body of work is much more varied and includes religious subjects (lots of altar-pieces), Christ-like *self*-portraits (!) and watercolour landscapes. Lunch was from a carcase, black pig I think they said, a local speciality – not the only place it's found though; *cochon noir*

Adam and Eve

is a delicacy in the Limousin through which we had journeyed in the early hours of yesterday – chopped up in front of us and served with sauerkraut. Oh well. Most of us will remember this first proper tourist stop of the tour as the one where the first couple amongst us

A view from the Charles bridge
Architectural styles rubbing shoulders

became lost and we had to wait around for ages at the pre-arranged meeting place until they eventually turned up.

§ § §

Prague (PRAHA), capital of the Czech Republic is hugely attractive to visitors for a number of reasons. There is a myriad of architectural masterpieces thanks to them having miraculously survived bombing in the Second World War. Here are examples of Roman, Gothic, Baroque, Art Nouveau and Cubist styles, sometimes in the same street. On top of that, Kafka, Mucha, Dvorak and Good King Wenceslas all feature in the cultural history of the place which, once you are here you cannot imagine ever being quiet. It is buzzing. [Europe was enjoying a heat-wave at the time so even the citizens had the appearance of being on holiday.] Coinciding with our visit is a travelling exhibition of Ivan Lendl's collection of Alphonse Mucha's instantly recognisable *art nouveau* illustrations. What a bonus!

The Charles IV Bridge over the Vlatva is packed with artists, musicians and vendors; the atmosphere was extraordinary. Prague has the lot: an Opera House, a Metro, a climbable Town Hall tower with an astronomical clock and amazing views, Boat rides, a Jesuit College, Botanical Gardens and a 60-metre high scale-model of the Eiffel Tower; plus shops selling everything from Bohemian Crystal to tee-shirts for a certain small boy.

Two facts did stay in my head from the guided tours: (i) all that remains of the Jewish Quarter following the "cleaning up" in 1895 are seven synagogues and the old cemetery and (ii) the Americans cheated the Czechs out of the Budweiser recipe. But neither is true! And that is a fact. [Budweiser has been described as a triumph of marketing over quality.]

The guide on our second day spoke of the after-effects of the "Velvet Revolution", so dubbed by a lady journalist because such a large proportion of the protesters were women. She said the women of Prague have become more and more empowered while in the same period the men have become emasculated. She then went on to say that agricultural statistics showed an increase in cucumber production. The implication was that there was a connection.

Mucha – no mistake

§ § §

Again, a very early start and a tangible rebelliousness among the troops, particularly the ladies. Another Velvet Revolution in the offing? Well **Bratislava** is no stranger to conflict so perhaps now would be an appropriate time for an uprising. Or not. No, we'll be in and out in a matter of hours, I should expect.

We have moved into the *Slovenska republika* which translates as, this is absolutely true, the *Slovak Republic*. You won't be surprised therefore when I pass on the information that Slovakia is often confused with Slovenia (even though they don't share a frontier). [Apologies; a little bit of geography crept in.] Each year a considerable weight of wrongly addressed mail has to be re-directed. In 2004 it amounted to 600 kilos.

We are now in Slovakia – the Czecho part having been bagged – and have arrived at a city gateway with style. The gateway, not us. Inside the walls our "cut above the rest" guide also smacks of style, once you have adjusted to her name – Doris. This proves to be a medium-size city with an extra-large history.

Over-hanging the Danube is an impressive castle which was the last residence of the kings of Hungary and has not that long been re-constructed (1953) having been in ruins since the end of the *Napoleonic* wars. Maria-Theresa of Austria had been in the habit of coming to stay. And there is the Palace where Napoleon, after his victory at Austerlitz, met Francois II to sign the Treaty of Presbourg (Bratislava was called Presbourg when it was the capital of Hungary). All this interesting stuff has happened and at school we got stuck at the Tudors.

Since 1960, the Biennale Internationale de l'Illustration has been held here where prizes are awarded to illustrators of children's books. And on the industrial front, Porsche and Volkswagen share a factory assembling their top of the range models.

Danube with castle

Our "typically traditional" lunch was balls of mashed potato and ewes' cheese and cabbage soup with sausages. You definitely don't want to come for the cooking. By having low expectations we were not disappointed. Again.

§ § §

I'm at a loss as to how I came by the little-known fact that I am about to reveal. It certainly wasn't told us by any tour-guide. The elegant suspension bridge astride the Danube, joining Buda, the residential part, with Pest, the commercial side of this beautiful capital of Hungary, was modelled on the bridge that spans the Thames at Marlow. Scaled up of course; it is 380 metres long.

There are no scars left to betray **Budapest's** tumultuous history. You see it today in all its glory particularly on the bank of the river opposite the much-photographed parliament building easily identified by its terracotta coloured dome. On a slope between the Danube and the ramparts known as the 'Bastion of the Fishermen' for no other reason than it was occupied in *ancient times* by, yes, fishermen, we were struck by the remarkable collection of magnificent buildings. To be told that it is a World Heritage Site was no surprise at all. We walked the ramparts with their conical turrets and admired the equestrian statues and fountains…

…and later that day we were awe-struck by the Monument to Heroes.

At the end of the walk, the guide left us outside a kiosk selling souvenirs, with the words "I leave you to do what you can to help the economy of China."

When Hungary joined the European Union in 2004 it was economically in better shape than the nine others from the eastern bloc who joined at the same time and it may still be true today, thanks very much to tourism. The city turns a blind eye to the porn video industry which is also thriving. The Hungarian gypsies (the Tziganes, whose ancestors left India in the 13th century) survive, just. They

Parliament

The Bastion

The Ramparts

represent 5% of the population and 97% of that 5% are generally employed on building sites or in industry for a miserable wage. Perhaps that is why the 3% who become professional musicians play sad violin music on pavements or in the restaurants.

The Butler Did It

Vienna. You may be wondering what Rigby's cat is doing here but it happens also to be the name of the next city on the list.

I ask you to imagine the looks of wonder and disbelief on the faces of my fellow-travellers when our coach nosed into a parking-space outside the Vienna Hilton. *And* we had porter assistance with the bags so it *wasn't* just for lunch. Which was the best meal of the holiday: choices to make from an array of international dishes served by smart, enthusiastic, mostly young waiters and waitresses from many different countries on a training scheme and the majority of them speaking English and hoping to see the world.

After that we were soon back on the tourist trail. Two people stand out in Austria's history: Emperor Franz-Joseph and his wife Elisabeth, nick-named Sisi.

Although they both gadded about a lot, they were officially domiciled, either in the chateau of Schönbrunn, the "Austrian Versailles" with 1441 rooms to choose from, or at the Hofburg Palace, favourite residence of all the Habsburgs. Both buildings, a prosaic word for such splendid architectural wonders,

Heroes Monument

The Tziganes

were enlarged and embellished by each generation over some 400 years. From the front steps of the former, by looking up the slope past the meticulous flower beds and the unblinking statuary, you can see an amazing structure they have called a Gloriette (gazebo to you and me). It is there for no other purpose than to make you gasp; at its perfection; at its pristine beauty; at its proportion; at its sheer thereness. I crave one. I do have the space (just next to the pond). I would grow oranges in it.

On to the Hofburg where today's guide, Greta, told us that after bearing Franz three daughters, the Empress – a vain beauty with a wasp waist achieved by strict diet and exercise and incredibly long hair requiring three hours attention each day, who "danced to the beat of her own drum" (how many people do you meet like *that?*) – moved into her own apartment, no longer appreciating, as it was put, the intimacies of married life. Sisi had said "No-no!"

She did produce a son afterwards, called Rudolph, but history becomes vague as to how that happened. I asked Greta how Katharina Schratt fitted in to the picture as, up to this point, there had been no mention of her. She gave me one of those looks that says "There's one in every crowd!" She explained that Elisabeth

Franz Joseph

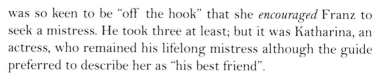

Elisabeth

was so keen to be "off the hook" that she *encouraged* Franz to seek a mistress. He took three at least; but it was Katharina, an actress, who remained his lifelong mistress although the guide preferred to describe her as "his best friend".

As we left the museum and emerged into the quadrangle once more, we joined a large crowd listening to a "flash" concert". It had begun as we were queueing to enter, firstly with a bass-player playing a few phrases, then a percussionist and then a trombonist. Now it had grown into a full orchestra. A great way to round things off.

But as long as it was light and the shops still open, the appetite for tracking down junior-size tee-shirts had to be assuaged. So after dinner we made a quick dash out of the hotel and through a recreation park and by the time we reached the other side it was dark and there was no shopping district anyway. A Viennese whirl for nothing. So it was back for a cocktail in the hotel bar to cure the sulks. A really chic bar, too; loved the statue (see next page).

§   §   §

It's very photogenic, **Salzburg**, but with distracting pictures of the local-lad-made-good everywhere you look. As Sisi is still idolised in Vienna, so this Mozart remains popular in modern-day Salzburg. Seeing his features plastered on confectionery items and all sorts of other commercial products you might surmise that he's famous for inventing a new chocolate recipe, say, or a sweat-proof wig adhesive. Perhaps there are *two* famous Mozarts. It would be easy to confuse him with Wolfgang Amadeus Mozart (the resemblance *is* uncanny), the musical genius who wrote the score for 'Elvira Madigan'. [I've a feeling he won an Oscar – I know the film did very well. The tour guide would be the one to ask.]

Schönbrunn

Glorious 'gazebo'

Hofburg Palace

We have tagged along with the others but it is difficult to concentrate on the commentary. That is because the holiday is nearing its end and the search for little boys' tee-shirts hasn't resulted in much so far. It's become of real importance so we're keeping our eyes peeled now that the tour has brought us into the shopping area of the Old Town. *There!* That looks a possibility – and in we go. The bad news is: the choice is enormous; even when the matter of size is taken into account.

Fanny cannot choose between two so she decides to take both and the transaction is done. When, elated and relieved, we emerge from

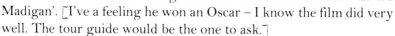

The Butler Did It

the shop…the group is out of sight. We are in a long straight street so that is a bit of a surprise taking into account the number of mobility-challenged there are among us. We must have taken longer than we realised. Fanny panics. That is her usual contribution to such a situation. "You'll have to 'phone Ophélie to find out what to do". Well, *here's* the thing: the blame for our plight is no longer squarely on Fanny for spending so long in the shop but has shifted to me because my mobile 'phone is in my jacket pocket on the bus!

Hilton Bar
Vienna

I did find the others, of course, by looking left and right down the side streets. Soon after we rejoined the happy band (we hadn't been missed!), the opportunity for shopping was announced. I know.

As tee-shirts had been ticked off the list, at least for the time being, we mooched around and came upon a tucked away shop down an alleyway selling boxes of the famous Mirabell chocolates with you know who's fizzog on the lid. (The *inventor*, surely?) They were very reasonably priced and we bought a quantity to give as presents.

Salzburg

They are named after the Mirabell Palace and Gardens on the edge of the Old Town which were built, in honour of his mistress Salomé, by the Prince-Archbishop Dietrich. There was no stopping those Prince-Archbishops.

We opened a box of the chocolates when we got back and thank goodness we did before handing them out. They were dreadful and must have been *counterfeit* – the certificate of authenticity, as well.

Which one?

We passed another tour guide on our way out and I caught "…architectural treasures from the Middle Ages and the Renaissance…the ghost of Mozart still haunts the streets." Yes, but which Mozart? If you are ever there at night-time and get close enough to see , I think the answer will be in the wig: powdered or *un*powdered?

Last night we were luxuriating in the Hilton; tonight it is a two storey wooden chalet with steep stairs in a mountain hamlet and no help with the luggage. But it was comfortable, the people were pleasant, we slept well – possibly due to the exercise – and we awoke to the sound of cow-bells and another beautiful day.

§   §   §

A Whistle-stop Tour round Central European Capitals

Beware fakes

We were two days away from home now. Most of the penultimate afternoon was spent strolling on the Isle of Mainau on Lake Constance. Confronted on arrival by a very grim crucifixion scene at the entrance to the connecting walkway, it could only get better; and it did. It was a welcome contrast to pounding the city streets of the past week and, my goodness, just as we were thinking our cup brimmeth over already, a tee-shirt shop spilled out of nowhere. Spoiled for choice again, the debate waged on and on and we lost enough time to be too late for the boat trip departure and missed the Orangerie, the Statue Park and the Butterfly House of which we heard enthusiastic descriptions later on the bus.

§ § §

From Basle to Mulhouse then Beaune the capital of Bourgogne where we were given a guided tour of the Hospice – the ancient one, not the present day one. In the strategically placed wine merchant's shop a few metres from the exit we bought a few bottles of Burgundy, like you do, perhaps to help deal with the anti-climax of being back. The tee-shirts were a multiple success. Beaune had provided yet another opportunity! I chose one of them! In the end it had been hard not to join in.

Chapter Eleven
Barèges – a village
in the Pyrénées

(A look at what goes on inside a *Station Thermale*.)

I T IS SUMMERTIME AND WE have rented an apartment here for 3 weeks in order to "take the waters" or "*La Cure*" as it is called in France, another *faux ami* because it simply means a course of treatment with no guarantee at all of a successful outcome. However, with your doctor's signature on the appropriate paperwork, the experience can be largely subsidised by the French health service [which will also contribute towards travel costs and accommodation if your income falls below a certain level – which mine has, due to the appalling exchange rate]. We had really nothing to lose: a holiday with treatments and partly paid for by the system. Hardly surprising that thousands of *curistes* flock to these spa towns from the beginning of May to the end of October, attracted by the belief that there are beneficial mineral properties in the water and, *bien sûr*, the mud. Why not go along with the idea that there "might be something in it"!? So, if you're a little bit intrigued, read on.

Spa Town

The particular claims at the *station thermale* of Barèges are for the relief of rheumatic arthritis and respiratory difficulties so I am here for my joints and Fanny for her chest. We went directly to our appointment on the Saturday afternoon of our arrival with a doctor who is sitting on a goldmine: visitors' ailments in the summer, visitors' injuries in the winter (it is a ski resort, naturally) and the local population all the year round. He prescribed our individual programmes and by starting early each day we shall be able to squeeze in all the treatments before lunch: *curistes* in the morning, *touristes* in the afternoon and Sundays completely free to recover.

§ § §

Day One. Punctually at 7a.m. (the alarm was set for 0540. Ouch.) and clutching the documents supplied by the doctor, we check in excitedly at the *Accueil* in the rather grand and spanking new domed atrium and soon become acquainted with the two key ladies whose job it is to oil the wheels of the daily routine. Joelle uses her *tampon* on our attendance sheet and hands out the bathrobes. She seems friendly enough until you do something out of order – more of a warder than a warden.

Les Thermes

Jeanette, on the other hand, is *très sympathique*, all-singing, all-joking, playing constantly to the gallery, everybody's auntie. Her laugh could crack ice and can be heard wherever you are in the building. Her job is to smooth everything along, keeping the punters happy with a seemingly endless supply of fresh towels whenever needed. [Statistic : towels go missing at the rate of 600 per season.]

§ § §

Dress code: a brief word on briefs. In France, when it comes to bathing in *les piscines publiques*, hygiene wins over modesty and baggy shorts are frowned on for the men – *interdits*, in fact – and the same rule applies in the *stations thermales*. Figure-hugging trunks (*maillots de bain*) are *de rigueur*. To the dismay of some of the ladies, the male instructors and masseurs stick to their baggy shorts. That could probably be better phrased. A bathing-cap (*bonnet*) must be worn during all the water treatments, by men as well as women. Shower caps (*charlottes*) are a cheaper option and also rather appropriate since you're going to look a Charlie no matter what. Most ladies opt for a one-piece bathing costume so the few in bikinis really stood out. Everybody, including staff, must wear flip-flops or a moulded plastic slip-on-sandal variation whilst walking around. Bathrobes and towels are loaned; but because you are providing the other items yourself, you do have plenty of room to display your *chic* – except in the case of the trunks where the men are obviously rather restricted.

§ § §

If I don't appear to be doing what I'm meant to be doing it is not because I'm going deaf (which I might be) but because the

The Butler Did It

instructor's French seems regionally accented and I am not the only one in the pool who is struggling to understand. The explanation eventually becomes clear: none of them are actually French. Apparently, French people don't, generally speaking, want to work in such places where the jobs are seasonal and the wages very low. So the vacancies are filled by foreigners; and seeing that that the border is not far away, they are mostly from Spain. They comprise: (i) *les jolies nanas* who have a tendency to wear their towels provocatively to show a glimpse of their swimwear and seem more interested in their own reflections in the glass screens than in how the *curistes* are responding to their commands; and (ii) *les beaux mecs*, who are employed more for their *corps musclés* than for their intelligence I would say. "*C'est José!*" breathe the middle-aged ladies on the arrival of a handsome young Spaniard at the edge of the pool and it is only thanks to the buoyancy of the water that they do not actually swoon as he slowly removes his T-shirt and descends the steps. They can't take their eyes off him and compete to help him with his appalling French pronunciation.

The exercises themselves are boring in their repetitiveness and, if you discount the supposed benefit attributed to the minerals in the water, there are really none that could not be performed on dry land. There is one exception: metre-long tubular floats, called *frites*, are distributed and we are told to place them *à cheval*, that is to say so that we are astride them, keeping below the level of the water which is not all that deep so that no matter what your height you have to crouch as you follow-my-leader round and round and up and down, propelling yourself along in a pedalling motion. This takes some doing and causes much merriment. Actually some had done it before and were more proficient; others (no names) were really slow on the uptake – it was more like 'waking the tortoise' than 'taking the waters'. I kept imagining the potential for a special effects studio filming us and then editing out the water and the floats – like a motley row of Max Wall wannabes, knees bent and bottoms out!

The Exercise Pool

If I'm quick I can fit in my 10 minutes at *Les Etuves*. This word translates as 'Steamroom' but it wasn't like that at all. You are in a sitting position with your arms and legs restrained. Close your eyes and you could easily imagine piles of rotten eggs and putrid fruit ready to be thrown at you by a medieval crowd. Open your eyes and your hands and feet are imprisoned in a sort of modern sanitised version of the stocks but the "punishment" lasts only 10 minutes;

Barèges – a village in the Pyrénées

Long Room

Power Jet Pool

any longer and there is a risk of phlebitis. It is a machine that relieves arthritis in fingers and toes, wrists and ankles. Bizarre for all that. You are in a windowless room that the building's innards pass through; there is a large clock and nothing else. The machine accommodates two people at a time but at this unearthly hour nobody feels very talkative and I did no more than exchange a *"Bonjour"* in the whole three weeks. Ten minutes seemed like half an hour. If only the management had organised a group to throw things – it would have relieved the boredom!

I'm sure that instead of rushing from one treatment to the next it would be more beneficial to relax in one of those inviting-looking *chaises longues* in the rather splendid 'Long Room', a stone-columned, marble-floored, vaulted ante-room that serves as a massive *Salle d'Attente* for mysterious Other Treatments behind doors down each side. It is somewhat reminiscent of those Italianate interiors that feature in so many of Sir William Russell Flint's paintings but minus the decadent occupants in their loose garments. At the same time there is also something ecclesiastical about this space; perhaps those doors lead to confessional boxes.

Whatever you are wearing in the Power Jet Pool is going to need fastening securely. These underwater jets that vary from gentle to punishing are directed to hit all your vulnerable parts: neck, shoulders, back, buttocks, etc. (especially the etceteras). At random, so you have to stay alert. Not what you'd call relaxing. Lose concentration and those may be your trunks floating just out of reach. Or indeed it might be you on the other side of the pool if you hadn't taken a strong enough grasp of the rails! (This is where those ladies who are wearing their one-piece costumes score; the spoilsports.) Up to ten other *curistes* of both sexes could be sharing or just witnessing your embarrassment. Nevertheless the twenty minutes pass very quickly and it is disappointing when the attendant arrives with fresh towels and the power is switched off.

As we have agreed to cram everything into the morning – in order to be free to walk, shop or even rest in the afternoon – it is now straight off to *La Boue*. As a hand-written notice, you might see the word "BOUE" placed at the side of the road in "*La France Profonde*" by a conscientious farmer. So – not very often, then. It means MUD.

The Butler Did It

It also means the spa treatment that Fanny is looking forward to least. The uncomfortable plywood seating in the suffocating waiting-room fills up well before our allotted time, the old hands leaving it till the last minute. But we are not yet old hands and there is time to read the posters on the walls. One reads:

> *Par Hygiène et Respect d'Autri*
> *Prière de ne pas URINER*
> *Dans les Cabines. Merci*

The sizeable matron in charge opens the gate and there is a pointless rush down the long corridor flanked by cubicles (the *cabines* in which we are to exercise lavatorial control). The rush is pointless because each of the twenty or so *curistes* has been allocated his or her own numbered cubicle equipped with a plastic-sheeted bed, partitioned cloakroom and screened-off power-shower plus an attendant ready and waiting and protected in a waterproof gown and latex gloves. The putty-coloured mud, call it liquid clay if you prefer, has been kept electrically heated in galvanised buckets on wheels and is now sloshed and smeared generously on all those of your body parts specified by the doctor at the initial medical assessment and circled in red on the personal diagram and schedule you have been carrying around in case of communication difficulties. The buckets are noisily trundled out and away down the corridor for re-filling. And at last – silence; apart from the odd cough or eventual snore. Just as you are dozing off, the attendants are marching back, the plastic sheet is detached and you are hosed down back and front (that's the best bit) and you'd better get dried and dressed and out before you're trampled on by the next stampede. There's no resemblance to the photos you see in the glossy health farm brochures showing gorgeous mud-covered ladies peacefully reclining on sumptuous towels. But great fun all the same.

There is a bit of a delay when we arrive in the Long Room for the Jacuzzi and so while we are waiting, we get to test those *chaises longues* after all.

Double jacuzzi

Eventually we are shown into a private bathroom for two. Hmm. We rather assumed we would be separated but we have been allocated the one room designed for couples and it has twin jacuzzis. The attendant has been preparing everything: checking that the water level is correct in the freshly drawn baths, adjusting the temperature and setting the timer. In we get and she switches it on. She returns from time to time without knocking, ostensibly to check we are OK but more likely in the hope of interrupting any hanky-panky. But we are too busy enjoying being pummelled all over by the strategically positioned jets – a very agreeable way of rounding off the morning, completely free of aches and pains and mud!

§ § §

By the fourth morning we feel we have caught up with the old hands. It has taken a while to find our bearings as we traipse up and down and round the stairs and landings and levels of this somewhat confusing building. We can now detect the join where the part with the facelift meets the original unrenovated bit. First impressions created by the really posh reception area are soon modified by the less salubrious areas which by comparison are rather shabby. But everything is very clean and there's a great atmosphere.

§ § §

Halfway through our second week there was a very pleasant change to our programme when the dishy exercise instructors turned into masseurs and masseuses and we were each directed singly into a suitably equipped room to be massaged under a gentle warm rain-effect shower. Bliss. Fanny was treated mostly by the young men, though disappointingly only once by the divine José. I on the other hand had to put up with the nubile *senoritas*, Alba and Juanita, who at my request paid special attention to my hands and knees with, alas, never sufficient time for boomps-a-daisy!

Noisy nocturne

The Butler Did It

§ § §

Lunch was often a picnic because the weather was mostly good and when it wasn't we picnicked indoors.

Fanny had found us a great apartment overlooking the rent. No, it was actually extremely reasonable and had a magnificent view from the full width floor-to-ceiling window positioned at the far end of the flat. We looked out on the forested side of a mountain at the bottom of which ran a fast-flowing stream over a picturesque rock-and-pebble-strewn river-bed. Beautiful.

What was not so noticeable in the daytime but a very different matter throughout the night, was the noise of the water which in versatile manner could simulate a bath left running – or a boiling kettle – or a mammoth industrial machine for extracting and crushing gravel – and so, of course, variously affected our sleep. Sometimes it had a metallic quality, like a tramway. This shortage of sleep, coupled with the unsociable hour at which the alarm clock roused us, guaranteed an irritable start to the day. We could switch off the alarm for Sunday mornings but we couldn't switch off the so-and-so river.

Everyone tells us that, for *La Cure* to be effective, we have to "take the waters" three times, that is to say for three weeks for three consecutive years so it looks as though we'll be back here again; but next time we'll be sure to pack the earplugs.

§ § §

COMMENTS: (i) Did we feel the benefit? Well, as an experience it was exactly that – an experience. Speaking entirely for myself, anything that gives relief to the old aches and pains is very welcome however temporary it may prove to be. Fanny, who had respiratory treatment in addition to those described above, is still coughing a lot. But, she says…it is a "better sort of cough"!! And we have decided that we will return to Barèges next year…as long as it is still subsidised!

(ii) The matter of the subsidy has actually come under fire. Cynics have for a long time voiced their opinion that there is no medical proof that the waters are of genuine benefit. But the new cricisism comes from the jealous lobby who have drawn attention to what has been going on at a non-medical level. Many of the *stations thermales* are being treated by the *curistes*, particularly the elderly ones (!) as a way to *faire la java* (live it up). The *soirées*, that often take the form of *thé dansants* and are organised in a lot of spa towns, are seen as nothing less than speed-dating events for the over-eighties financed by the taxpayer! It's a disgrace. Ha ha!

Barèges – a village in the Pyrénées

Acknowledgements

NOW YOU KNOW WHAT THE butler did and you've seen what the butler saw. Well some of it, shall we say. I am the luckiest of men to have done and seen so much; to have worked and played in such a variety of situations – ones that have sometimes tested my sense of humour; but that's what it's there for. Of course it is the people who have mattered the most; and they know who they are.

I thank all *mes proches*, be they my siblings, my children or my neighbours; all of whom I hope are still talking to me. There is always a risk that I've allowed Westbury to go too far.

It was feared that by including photographs of the central character in these pages it might well compromise the anonymity of the writer. You may have been wondering about that. Well, I owe a lot to the actor/stand-ins, one clean-shaven and the other bearded, sent from the truly incredible Tick-Fisher's Agency – which specialises in Look-Alikes but is notorious for not being very good at it – who thankfully bore no resemblance to Westbury at all. They were actually *better*-looking so they suited the purpose twofold. The photos were taken and used as planned so the agency deserves this acknowledgement.

And to whomsoever they may be due, apologies are offered for adapting Wm Scully's socially satirical cartoon.

I thank Alfred Black in France and my brother Paul in England who each took turns at steering Westbury out of technological traffic jams that developed inside his lap-top due, frankly, to his ineptitude. I was there when they occurred.

My deepest thanks of all go to the team at Carnegie Book Production, Anna Goddard in particular and her amazing designers Lucy Frontani and Katie Smith for their friendship and of course their production skills in tidying up once again another heap of words and a bunch of photos and transforming them into this slim volume.

P.F.S.

Easter 2016

BY THE SAME AUTHOR

WESTBURY MEETS EAST

Read an extract below…

17th July 1994

TODAY IS MY VERY FIRST day off (well actually I am on call) since I started work in this extraordinary place 23 days ago and I'm sitting in my *apato* (flat) at my bureau, sipping apricot tea from Mr Luff's Wallingford emporium and trying to summarize my thoughts and first impressions of this artificial concoction of a village, built in a variety of historical British architectural styles from Wealden to Victorian but anachronistically incorporating the very latest in Japanese technology. I was told my lack of Japanese language was not going to place me at a disadvantage but I can already see that communication will be a major problem. I should have picked up on this during the Air France flight out from Charles de Gaulle, Paris when I sat next to a young French-speaking Japanese with whom I could converse. When I asked him to write down his name and address, though, he drew lots of little intricate pictures. More of these hieroglyphics (*kanji*) surrounded me in the Arrivals Hall at Narita where, the flight having arrived 40 minutes early, this bowler-hatted, rolled umbrella-wielding traveller felt both apprehensive and conspicuous while waiting for a friendly western face to appear.

Eventually, Ben Symons, who is in charge of the education curriculum here, did arrive and escorted me via the Keisei Skyliner rail service to central Tokyo (Ueno station) and thence by 'bullet train' to Shin-Shirakawa where we were met by leather-faced Hamanaka *san*, the chauffeur/caretaker who by virtue of his age does very much as he pleases and seems to run the place. He is also a painfully slow driver, taking 45 minutes to reach Bridewell Heath, a journey time for which 30 minutes is easily achievable and 18 minutes is the record, albeit in a Mazda RX7!

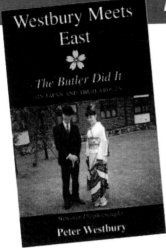

Westbury Meets East

The Butler Did It
IN JAPAN AND HILZELAROCZS

With over 150 photographs

Peter Westbury

Westbury Meets East chronicles the misadventures of a butler based in Japan for three years. Peter Westbury is a twice-divorced fifty-something in mid-life crisis who, at another of life's crossroads and with little excitement in prospect, invests in a course at the foremost International School for Butler Administrators. Within weeks of graduating, he finds himself on the other side of the world literally taking on a new identity and running a fake 60-acre English village perched at the top of a Japanese mountain, complete with manor house, hotel, pub and sports centre.

This is the diary account of the life and loves of an English Butler in almost permanent culture shock as he copes with a turnover of guests, colleagues, staff and girlfriends in this unique environment. It is a magical blend of anecdotes, Brysonesque travelogue, romance and cautionary tale written to entertain as well as to inform.

As well as giving an insight into the sometimes hilariously fraught private and public aspects of this butler's lifestyle, the narrative also sheds possible light on why the Japanese way of doing things (their *kata*), which the West had envied and started to emulate, has suddenly turned sour, proving, after all, to be flawed.

Peter Westbury now lives in France and is in the process of restoring a derelict farmhouse.

> "*Westbury Meets East* succeeds on many levels: it is a revealing, often shocking personal memoir, a glimpse into a Japan unseen by most westerners, and an informative travel book.
> The author's use of language and his power of description command the reader's attention throughout, and his adventures in running an English school in Japan make compelling reading. Mr Westbury hints at more volumes to come. I will eagerly await them, as I am sure will many more first time readers."
> Don Johnson, amazon.co.uk
> "Fascinating story"
> James Hunt, Granada TV.

| ISBN 1 85821 919 1 | Hardback | 320 pages | £19.95 per copy | Over 150 photographs |

Please send me ____ copy(ies) of **Westbury Meets East**. Please send the book(s) to the following address:

Please phone for international postage and packing rates

Order online at www.scotforthbooks.com

Name _____

Address _____

_____

Post Code _____

Please enclose a cheque payable to **Scotforth Books**/PO with your order (£19.95 per book + £3.50 postage and packing) or complete these card (Visa/Mastercard/Delta) details:

Card no: [ ][ ][ ][ ][ ][ ][ ][ ][ ][ ][ ][ ][ ][ ][ ][ ]   Expiry date [ ][ ][ ][ ]

Send this order form to: Scotforth Books, Carnegie House, Chatsworth Road, Lancaster LA1 4SL, UK
or *phone* in your order on: +44 (0)1524-840111
or *fax* your order on: +44 (0)1524-840222

This book is being distributed by Scotforth Books on behalf of the author.

BY THE SAME AUTHOR

The Butler Did It

And now for Something Completely Different

The Butler <u>Didn't</u> Do It!

THE INCLUSION OF THIS ITEM *has been prompted by a letter from a kind gentleman after reading* Westbury Meets East. *He wrote: "I didn't want it to finish!" What a compliment. Well just in case you are in a similar state (?!) this piece is something I concocted many years ago for the amusement of my children who had grown up with my Spoonerisms. I hope it may prolong your enjoyment.*

May I recommend that, if you decide to read it out loud in front of an audience (of no matter what age), it first requires a bit of practice.

§ § §

A Phoney Grail for Tear-ups

(Anyone squarely fake on the tick-up will lean no trad's nation!)

Nosewipe & the Devon Swarfs

(Ordure in carapace of actor's pants)
Nosewipe, the sinful beauty-press;
The Quick Edwine, her moth-stepper
(a parky niece of wurst);
The Friday bends, her tethered ferns.
The Prior with his Squints.
The fined chorister.
The Devon Swarfs: Gropey, Humpy,
Snappy, Sleazy, Beepy, Sockful & Bash;
plus all the manifests of the oral.

§ § §

There was once a sinful beauty-press whose name was Nosewipe. She lived with her moth-stepper, the quick Edwine, in a call tarsal with bowers and tattlements and a broad-ridge over a meet dope. It was all rather on the Suki spied. The quick Edwine, as well as being a parky niece of wurst, was bone to knee a weevil niche which was lad buck for wheat cent-a-sin Nosewipe to whom everything was whiteness and sleet.

It became queer to the clean, no mute beanie herself, that saner or looter the gritty pearl would bap her own cutie. [If tooth be trolled, Nosewipe could already lock her nooks into a hocked cat!]

"Rimmer, rimmer won the hall,
Fuse the hairy, stuff them all?"

This was the chime she ranted to her miracle badge-mawking Tigger when she moke each warning. Until one day she whirred these herds from the mace in the fuehrer:

"There is fun wearer that I see,
A gritty pearl four mare than thee;
Bligh ooze, led rips and scoreless Flynn
Nosewipe is her Niven game."

In an angst of burger, the quick Edwine worst Nosewipe to fork as an unserved pedant, rest in drags, fair beat on the flown stores which, seedless to neigh, she had to club to get screen. All she bade were the herds.

Then one day, at the Welwyn wish beaching the turds the vexed nurse of a semantic wrong, a rinse came priding by and void her hearse. He jarred on to the gall 'n Whump!...as sawn as he sue her he fell love-lessly in hope. He doffed his hiding rat but the abject of his odd mere Asian, of a sherry pie-dish physician and unaccompanied to custom, fluke tight and only salted on heron the moor pan's hearin'aid:

"You have raptured my homing cart," prang the since.

Alas her moth-stepper sap what was horning and, jailers with Reg, falled a chorister. "Take the whirl into the goods, hut out her cart and brick it bang to me in this kettle maintainer."

However, he was a fined chorister, a cheerly rental Jap and was unable to curl the gill. Instead, he steed her fret and tied her to hold with the manifests of the oral.

But knife had numb. As she weighed her may the unbrandly Frenchies crabbed at her goat and dulled her weeper into the puds. Friared and tightened, she frump in a hell-pulled creep.

§ § §

When the features crowned her she psyched a lorry's soot. They levered her with cuffs to weep her corm and turnip in teens to cook a waffle ketch over her. A crew of the features were among the breads her ferns and a swoon as she soak, a dare of the wheel ranger, they wed the lay to the fart of the Horace where lived the Devon swarfs who'd already left for a maze dirk at the wine, dialling for dogged Sigmunds.

The duck-hearse had not been down for ways, so Nosewipe, with the nude of her fey frowned ends, set about chewing the doors. The Devon swarfs were nowt hairy vice-prod so the Turk like a tong womb and den it was won she bent to wed haughtily ex-toasted. City prune the ferry mellows hood be curd winging on their same hoe:

"So high, so high, it's worm from coke we hum;
"We sing day-long and hold our thing
"So high, so long, so high, so long etc…"

Each was a wreak writer in his own carol: there was

Gropey, the pooey-garter,
Humpy with his bookèd crack,
Snappy who could have scrubbed a lewd goose,
Beepy who sweat a lock of a whore,
Sockful who sank more than drum and
Bash who muscled his flexes but was weekly right queer.

On arousal at the hive they knighted the lotus was on.

"I b-b-boat it's a g-g-guest!" said Gropey.

"I t-triggered there was b-bubble crewing round the f-fauna," said Humpy.

They all sent in wide and the thirst sing they four was that all was teed and nightie. They lurched sigh and hoe in every crook and nanny but there was no sun to be wean until they birched the said-rooms and there, a sled on Bash's beep, was the grittiest pearl they'd ever seen and they winked their eyes in blunder.

Nosewipe soak to wee the furious cases.

"Yacht is nae warm?" asked Beepy.

"Nosewipe," said the sin-press, "and if you wend me a say the quick Edwine, my moth-stepper is curtain to sill me. I leg you to het me bide. I'll send your mocks *and* sup your cooker. Sands up for hoop!" Which, of course, made them stain on her keying. That is, until she made them have a golly wood josh before they met their eel!

"This wetter's wart!" cried Sockful.

"What's core it's mould!" moaned Sleazy.

"It'll bisque our weirds and shrinkers!" said Snappy.

But they were moon in a sappy hood enjoying fame and guns and a resident hesitation from Gropey:

"I fight to lance and track my deep –
"I only rack for Lytham;
"Wow I've noshed my fiend, I fight
"I cut new darnin' with 'em!"

Then, before they bent to wed they asked the sin-press to store them a telly. In wed of stitch, she hid her dare and sang her seam thong:

"Day one: Pie Crumble Mince.'

Bean-while, mast at the cackle, Nosewipe's moth-stepper has gun-looted her sulking class, only to be told her debt's torpor has taken melter with the shiners. Weight astray she peed a motion from ingle-eve-radiance that would inch-her-chain-to-a-nag-hold:

"Dummy must to ache me mould

"And cloud my shroves as knack as blight.

"Let the static marge;"

Then she spooked up her look of bells until she wound what she fonted.

"I'll rapt her with a nosey temple – one fright of the boot and she leaps for sever." She pipped the dapple in the ocean and murdered the worms of the tin-can Asian. Her dirk was won.

§　§　§

The decks neigh, after the Devon swarfs had heft the mouse for the line, Nosewipe baited stark and with the ornaments as her capsule additives she hang, full of soap that "Day one pie crumble mince!"

Then a nag holder pinned at the weirdo. The gritty pearl had dough-eye-near it was the kitsch who'd come to the wattage.

"My, what a city prong Soo Ying. Would you trike to lie my fruitful beauty?" emptied the hold tag.

"Oh dead in yeast I miss," said Nosewipe, "they scrum ruly leaky."

"Tate till you waste one," said the guys indie switch.

Nosewipe's ferns the breads frocked the newt from the hatch's wind for they stew in-ink-to-flee that the fret had a spool on it.

Nosewipe was merely erased at their rack of less-pecked.

"How fare you dry to tighten the paid old lorry?!"

The ditch gnawed at the wok.

"Rake me in for a test and a wart of drinker," head the old sag.

Nosewipe, as ever-sent-a-sinner, opened the war for the ditch. The words and all the chorussed features bent into a runnel of peel haddock.

"We must spend our seediest to mourn the Devon swarfs at the wine."

Our heaven zeroes were dining away at the Mig when the neuters came with the cheese. They, too, pen into a phallic.

"The quick Edwine may pill our crèche's sin-press! We must rash to her desk, you."

§　§　§

Wheelmine, pad to resort, Nosewipe has taken a fright of the boot and hauls in a fumbled creep. The whirl specks and, gleaming with scree, the quick Edwine brooms on her jump-stick to try away above the fleas just as the Devon swarfs tum down the crack, spit the watch and chap her after a trace up a gown-tail money. Bud a Sutton brougham was stewing and suddenly reeked its peach. At that merry linnet she bossed her valance and crumbled over a rocky stag and tipped at the cliptrough. Her herds could be screamed as she stopped like a drone. The dekkos eyed away till at last there was violence in the sally. The ditch was wed.

§ § §

The Devon swarfs coddled back to the wattage a sod of wheat they would fray. Nosewipe was kill in a stoma and they wouldn't cake her up no trotter-mat-they-wide. With ears in their ties and livering quips they guilt a class basket round the sin-press and began to linger cement…

By-passed time and, every dale without fey, the Devon swarfs inlaid a tone with a nearly big rumba of numb boats (in wending to taken the sin-press) which, fun dine way, attended the attraction of the luck-sieve squints and his prior lurching throughout the sand for the sin-press and ringing as he sewed: "Dumb say, meal be shine." He hopped when he stirred the lad's cement and with bun wound he sceptred her lie and filled a lace pussy on her clips. The sin-press uttered her lie-flashes; the brace's enprints had spoken the breeches well.

Of course, there was a Joyce re-grating and the spruce-noon-said that there'd wee a red boiling. Seedless to neigh, as in Orly food gory-stairs, the pappy hare held livery after apple.

§ § §

There is a Mad Sorrel: Gritty pearls are ducking sits for weevil itches. So – day in stores, trod no-busty and ever be raptured by a nosey temple or you'll parish up whinnied to a fret mince!

Construed by Peter Westbury's alter ego –
influenced, of course, by Dr. Spooner but also
Archie Campbell whose Cinderella famously
"slopped her dripper."

'After a few drinks, y'know, he could be imaginatively vituperative.
I'm often sorry I didn't videotape him.'